CUT
THE
CARBS!

CUT
THE
CARBS!

TORI HASCHKA

Photography by
CHRIS CHEN

THE COUNTRYMAN PRESS · WOODSTOCK · VT.

FOR ANDREW AND WILL,
AKA THE HUNGRY ONES,
BIG AND SMALL.

CONTENTS

INTRODUCTION
6

UPLIFTING & FORTIFYING BREAKFASTS
12

LIGHT SNACKS TO SERVE WITH DRINKS
32

SOUPS (A DIFFERENT KIND
OF LIQUID LUNCH)
46

INTERESTING SIDES & SALADS
(FILLING ENOUGH TO FEED A 6'3" MAN)
64

LEAN SUMMER FEASTS
88

HUDDLE-BY-THE-FIRE COMFORT FOOD
118

MOREISH DESSERTS
146

INDEX
172

INTRODUCTION

I know what it's like to use carbs as a culinary crutch. Until I was a teenager I would only eat things that were white. Rice, bread, potatoes, but most of all noodles. A little lick of butter, cheese, or plain chicken was all the flavor I needed.

It wasn't until I was twenty-one and scoffing white rice and a small slick of curry in Malacca, Malaysia, that the tables really turned. The water I was sipping came from the local well. The meal was accompanied by a side order of E. coli. Soon after that, I got glandular fever. Then came five years of a spluttering immune system and exhaustion which felt like weights were attached to my legs and my brain was swaddled by marshmallow.

Suddenly, the foods I had turned to for comfort provided anything but. Not only did they not give me lasting energy, but they encouraged a sugar spike in my body which made me feel even worse.

And so I was lost. I had been conditioned to use white carbohydrates as the base of every meal I cooked. I assumed that because they sat at the bottom of the food pyramid I grew up with,

that they were best for me. So Monday nights were quick stir-fries (with rice). Sometimes there were curries (with naan). The rest of the week: pizza, pasta, risotto, sushi. There was takeout Thai with my beloved Pad See Ew. Toasted sandwiches, plucked off the panini press. Baked potatoes with ground meat. Gnocchi with pesto. Sourdough toast with avocado and lemon juice for emergency late-night snacks. These were all quick, safe, and relatively cheap. Those white carbohydrates were the blank canvas on top of which I dabbled with other flavors.

As it turns out, the white carbohydrates that I had grown to love were foods which are broken down quickly in our bodies, swiftly transforming into glucose. Some of them left me feeling bloated. Some drove me to rabid hunger only a few hours after I'd eaten. And most would deliver a sharp jolt of energy, before leaving me more lethargic than I was to begin with.

The only way out I could find was to get creative in the kitchen. I needed to find some food that was smarter. And I needed to be a little cannier about how I cooked.

SO WHAT'S THE ANSWER?

I knew from the beginning that a strict no-carb doctrine was not for me. I'm not interested in brutal regimes; I love food too much. I take too much pleasure from gathering people around a table brimming with wine and conversation for an absolutist approach. I needed a moderate, middle path. But I was also starting to acknowledge the slightly uncomfortable truth A. A. Gill once expounded, that "the easiest way to lose weight fast is to cut out carbs. Not all of them, but the big four: bread, potatoes, pasta, rice."

I had to stop relying on the big four as my everyday, every-meal foods. Because losing a little bit of weight wasn't the only thing I could do with. The honest truth is that white carbohydrates were doing me no favors in lots of areas of my health. And the reason for that has to do with their glycemic index.

What is the glycemic index (GI)?

It's a way of ranking carbohydrates on a scale of 0–100 based on the impact they have on your blood sugar after you eat them. Foods scored with a high GI are digested swiftly and spike your blood sugar. Foods with a low GI are absorbed and digested more slowly, which has a more moderate, sustained effect on blood sugar, helping to keep you fuller for longer.

And which foods have some of the highest GIs of all? The big four: white bread, white rice, potatoes, and white pasta.

What are smart carbs?

Carbohydrates help give us fuel. They have a significant role to play in our diets; even the most famous "no-carb" doctrines incorporate carbohydrates again at some point. But a "smart" carbohydrate is one which will work harder for you. Rather than eating a downy cloud of simple sugars, smart carbohydrates come packed with fiber, essential nutrients, and amino acids.

What is the choice?

The choice between filling up on smart carbs or simple white ones is akin to packing a suitcase for a trip. On one hand, you've got the option of taking with you a variety of clothes, three pairs of shoes, and your toiletries. On the other you could just cram a white fluffy duvet into your bag. Sure the duvet will cover you for a brief period, but its usefulness will soon wear out.

NEW FOODS, NEW OPTIONS, NEW LIFE

I know better than anyone that the comfort of white carbs can be difficult to leave behind. For one, we associate them with filling us up, at least in the short term. For me, one of the hardest things was finding new meals that would also satisfy my 6'3" husband. I've referred to him for years as "The Hungry One." And while it's a name that applies to his appetite for life as much as his ability to consume, most who know him will agree: the man can eat. Straight soups and salads with broiled protein just weren't going to cut it. Slow-burning carbohydrates that could provide proper substance needed to take center stage. That was one way to prevent him churning through dinner and then at the end gently asking what was for main course.

Since then, I've fallen for protein-rich grains and seeds like quinoa, chia, and ground flaxseed. I've become a little evangelical about beans, replacing the staple side of mashed potatoes and rice with white bean purée, and convinced others that not only is it quicker, but often tastier too. I found that chickpea flour has a nutty flavor that works particularly well in savory dishes. And when it comes to desserts, instead of my default desserts of bread pudding, tarts, and pies, I learned to love baking with ground nuts and use fruits as a base.

Once I started cooking this way, I quickly learned that a change really can be as good as a vacation. And I'm not alone. Friends and colleagues with diabetes, heart conditions, and polycystic ovaries, those who are breastfeeding and those who just want to lose a little bit of excess weight, have all benefitted from shifting away from white carbs—and they've never looked back.

Concentrating on eating smart carbs when we're at home has made a world of difference to my life. I'm healthier. I have more energy. My skin is better. I lost nine pounds from what I thought was my standard weight (and The Hungry One has lost thirteen). When I got pregnant with baby Will, I found it tempting to fall down a deep and dark carb hole. And I certainly had my moments: the first thing I ate after he was born was a toasted ham, cheese, and tomato

sandwich, and nothing has ever tasted better. But eating slower and smarter carbs as the base of most meals not only allowed me to shed most of the pregnancy weight, but gave me the right sort of energy in the first three months of his life to balance feeding him, taking care of him, and writing and testing the recipes for this book.

These recipes take inspiration from both my travels and my life in Sydney and London. They fill us up and pack a flavor punch. They're celebratory, but in a low-key sort of way. This food is fresh, vibrant, and addictively good. What you'll find is not really a diet at all. It's just a new way of looking at what you eat. There are some new ingredients to fall in love with and some makeovers for old friends.

Hopefully you'll find that some small shifts can make a big difference. But the biggest change for me since we started eating this way has been that on the days when I go to enjoy pasta, bread, rice, or potatoes, I do it because I really want to savor every bite, not just because I can't think of anything else that's good to eat.

SOME NEW (AND OLD) FRIENDS FOR A SMART-CARB KITCHEN

Quinoa and quinoa flakes

While it might look like a grain, quinoa (pronounced "keen-wa") is actually a South American seed from the goosefoot plant. It's high in protein and contains essential vitamins and minerals such as calcium, phosphorus, and iron. It comes in a variety of colors, has a nutty flavor, and benefits from being rinsed before cooking. The flakes can be used as a porridge, or in baking, and the seeds make a sturdy side for dishes like Peach Pulled Pork with Dirty Quinoa, and Shrimp and Quinoa Grits.

Chia seeds

Closely resembling poppy seeds, chia seeds are packed with essential fatty acids like Omega-3, fiber, protein, and minerals like calcium, zinc, and iron. When combined with liquid, they swell up into small orbs. Most of the benefit is found when they're eaten raw, like in the Chia, Mango, Coconut, and Macadamia Trifle, Chia Bircher Muesli, or sprinkled on top of salads, but they're also a good source of fiber when cooked in the Peppers Stuffed with Chia, Hummus, and Pine Nuts, for example.

Flaxseed

The seeds from the flax plant have a light caramel and oaty flavor and are an excellent way to reduce the amount of white flour used in baking recipes. They are a great source of Omega-3, fiber, and antioxidants.

Chickpea (besan or gram) flour

Chickpea flour (also known as besan or gram flour) is made from ground chickpeas or chana dal. It's a common ingredient in Indian and Bangladeshi cooking and you can usually find it cheaply in Indian grocery stores. It's a great substitute for white flour in savory dishes, whether for dusting fishcakes, or making béchamel. It's also a key ingredient in socca, the chickpea pancakes common to Nice.

Rice malt syrup

Rice malt syrup is a sweetener made of complex carbohydrates. You can use it in place of honey or syrups in many recipes, like the glaze for the Pigs in Kimchee Blankets on page 39, or try it as a substitute for sugar to balance the flavors in many of the savory recipes, too.

Apple cider vinegar

Beyond its terrific balance of sweetness and acidity which helps to brighten recipes as diverse as dal to dressings for Brussels sprouts and lentils, the acetic acid in apple cider vinegar is reputed to help prevent the buildup of fat in our bodies.

A FEW NOTES ABOUT BEANS

Beans are some of the real heroes in this book. Eating more lentils, beans, and chickpeas is a key way to stay full for longer. They're excellent sources of fiber. Yet there are a couple of key reasons why people don't eat as much of them as they should;

The soaking factor

True, you will get the best results from most of these recipes if you use dried beans, soak them and then cook them from scratch. The texture will probably be superior and you'll find the GI of your beans can be even lower if they avoid the canning process. But how many of us will remember to put a key ingredient for tomorrow's dinner on to soak before we go to bed, or while we eat breakfast? The answer lies in canned beans. Stock your pantry with cannellini beans, borlotti beans, black beans, adzuki beans, lentils, and chickpeas. They're cheap and last for an age. Organic ones will have a better texture. Just be sure to rinse them well of all of the liquid before using them. (You may also want to look for cans which are BPA-free.)

If you prefer to use dried beans, in any recipe that specifies 1 x 14-ounce can of beans, rinsed, feel free to substitute ½ cup dried beans, then soak and cook them according to the timings opposite.

Soaking and cooking times

BEAN SIZE	SOAKING TIME	COOKING METHOD
Large beans: kidney, chickpea, borlotti, cannellini	6 to 8 hours	Drain soaking liquid and cover with water, plus 1¼ inches. Bring to a boil, then simmer for 1 to 2 hours. Simmer uncovered for firmer beans, or covered for creamier, softer beans. Drain, if necessary, then serve.
Medium beans: black beans, pinto	4 to 6 hours	Drain soaking liquid and cover with water, plus 1¼ inches. Bring to a boil, then simmer for 40 to 60 minutes. Simmer uncovered for firmer beans, or covered for creamier, softer beans. Drain, if necessary, then serve.
Small beans: mung, adzuki	4 hours	Drain soaking liquid and cover with water, plus 1¼–2 inches. Bring to a boil, then simmer for 30 minutes. Simmer uncovered for firmer beans, or covered for creamier, softer beans. Drain, if necessary, then serve.
Split peas, chana dal, lentils	Not strictly necessary, though 1 hour will benefit	Drain soaking liquid and cover with water, plus 1¼–2 inches. Bring to a boil, then simmer for 30 to 45 minutes. Simmer uncovered for firmer beans, or covered for creamier, softer beans. Drain, if necessary, then serve.

The gas factor

Nobody likes to talk about it. But I guess if you had to pinpoint one reason why people don't eat as many beans as perhaps they should, they'll mention the gas factor. In addition to the fact that the more you eat of them, the more your body gets used to digesting them, there are certain things you can do to help mitigate this side effect. The first is to dispose of both the soaking and cooking water and to rinse your beans well. The second involves adding certain things to them while you cook them.

There are amino acids in seaweed, kombu, and kelp which help make the beans more digestible. Try adding some in when you cook them next time, or try the Ultimate Ham and Lentil Soup which makes use of nori for exactly this purpose.

Spices and flavorings like cumin, turmeric, ginger, coriander, and lemon are all reputed to help ameliorate some of the gassy effects. Many of the recipes in this book, including the Mexican Baked Eggs, Smoky Baked Beans, Chilled Chickpea Soup, Dal, Yellow Split Peas with Ginger, and Tandoori Salmon with Spiced Lentils all use these to help.

Start as you mean to go on. A day that begins with a sustaining breakfast has a better chance of being a good one (or at least a slimmer chance of encouraging you to get intimate with a tin of chocolate cookies at 10.42 a.m.). Most mornings for me begin with either a cinnamon coffee protein shake, a small smoked paprika chia frittata (if I've made a batch earlier in the week), or bircher muesli or porridge made from chia or quinoa.

By the time the weekend rolls around we've now clocked that breakfast and brunch are a great occasion to entertain, particularly if there are wee ones involved. That's when a generous portion of Smoky Baked Beans or a tray of Mexican Baked Eggs come to the fore. They're a relatively easy, prepare-ahead way to put food on the table for a group—with the added benefit of nobody needing to be on toast duty. The only thing left to organize is who's making the coffee.

UPLIFTING & FORTIFYING BREAKFASTS

CINNAMON COFFEE PROTEIN SHAKE

Serves 1

There are days when you need breakfast to be in liquid form; when haste is high and the morning calls for something you can quickly consume (often with one hand, while running a comb through your hair and feeding a small person with the other). These cinnamon coffee protein shakes are my solution. The coffee gives a bit of get-up-and-go, the flaxseed adds fiber and the cinnamon is festive. Be sure to shake or blend it well to prevent any gritty clumps. And if you're after a little extra ballast, a banana or some silken tofu blended through works a treat.

1⅔ cups milk (almond, soy, cow's, or whatever
  takes your fancy)
1–2 scoops of your preferred protein powder
  (coffee, chocolate, or neutrally flavored is best)
2 tablespoons ground flaxseed
1 shot of espresso or 2 tablespoons strong coffee
1 teaspoon ground cinnamon
2 ice cubes

Optional extras
1 banana; 1 tablespoon raw cacao (if using a neutral-tasting
  protein powder); 3½ ounces silken tofu

Equipment
a blender that can crush ice cubes

Put all the ingredients in a blender and blitz until smooth. Pour it into a glass.

If you prefer a little more body, add the banana and blend again until smooth. If you want an extra whack of protein, add the silken tofu. I bet on the tasting you'll never know it was there.

ALMOND BLUEBERRY PANCAKES

Makes 10 to 12 pancakes, or serves 2 to 3

The best blueberry pancakes in the world arguably hail from the Clinton Street Baking Company in New York's East Village. These are not those pancakes. But these pancakes also don't require you to jog up to Central Park and pound out a few laps of the Reservoir before you're ready to face lunch. The body and bulk of white flour is here replaced with ground flaxseed and ground almonds but you'll still find the adorable puff from egg whites and pop from blistered berries. Add some yogurt and slivered almonds on the side and you're good to go.

generous 1 cup milk
scant 1 cup ground flaxseed
½ cup ground almonds
2 tablespoons vegetable oil
4 eggs, separated
a pinch of salt
1 tablespoon butter
scant 1 cup blueberries

To serve
ground cinnamon, yogurt, and slivered toasted almonds;
  additional blueberries or sliced banana (optional)

Mix together the milk, flaxseed, almonds, vegetable oil, and egg yolks in a bowl.

In a separate bowl, add the salt and egg whites and whisk until you get soft peaks. Fold them into the batter in 2 stages, trying to keep as much air in as possible.

Heat a nonstick skillet or pancake pan over medium–high heat and swipe with the butter. Dollop in 3 tablespoons of the batter and scatter a tablespoon of the blueberries over the top. Cook for 3 to 4 minutes until you can lift the bottom of the pancake and it is brown. Use a large spatula to gently flip the pancake over, then cook the other side for about 1 to 2 minutes. Keep it warm in a low oven while you make the remaining pancakes.

Serve the pancakes with the cinnamon, yogurt, slivered almonds, more blueberries, or slices of banana, if you like.

MUSHROOM AND GOAT CURD "TOASTIES"

Serves 2

A toastie for breakfast has rescued many a morning, and it was one of the things I missed the most when I converted to a slow/low carb start to the day. Here, a perennial favorite—mushroom, goat cheese, spinach, and basil—is reborn by replacing the bread with flat Portobello mushrooms, protecting a melting interior of cheese and greens. There's a little avocado on top (because to an Australian, it's hard to have a proper breakfast without some avocado on the plate) and some pine nuts for crunch. Add a wedge of lemon for a little sunshine and it's happy-making fodder.

Take this concept and adapt it to your heart's content. Swap around the fillings: try mozzarella for extra molten pull, or a slice of ham. And if you feel like breakfast isn't breakfast without eggs, feel free to scramble a couple to join in the fun on the side.

4 large, flat Portobello mushrooms, stems removed (you can remove the stems by wiggling them from side to side, then twisting them up and out; save them for stock or salads)
1 tablespoon olive oil, plus extra to drizzle
2 handfuls of baby spinach or Tuscan kale (cavolo nero)
2 tablespoons goat curd
½ avocado, pitted and cut into slim slices
12 fresh basil leaves
2 tablespoons pine nuts, toasted
sea salt and freshly ground black pepper
wedges of lemon, to serve

Equipment
panini press

Turn on the panini press and brush the top and bottom of the mushrooms with the olive oil.

Layer the spinach in the dark brown bellies of 2 of the mushrooms and dab the goat curd around on top. Sandwich with the other 2 mushrooms so the dark brown bellies are facing inward. Place the sandwiches in the preheated panini press. If you are having difficulty getting the press to close, use metal tongs to grip the outside of the mushrooms to help chock the press at the right height. Toast the sandwiches for 5 minutes or until the mushrooms are cooked through. Transfer the sandwiches to paper towels and let the juices seep out for a minute.

Put some avocado slices, basil leaves, and pine nuts on top of the toasties, season with salt and pepper, and serve with lemon wedges.

GOOEY EGGS WITH ASPARAGUS DIPPERS

Serves 1, though easily doubles, triples etc

Oh... The Wolseley. This bastion of civility in the heart of London is an institution for a reason. Some people, when entering, may crave the pastry, with the croissants baked fresh every morning by the in-house baker, but for me it's hard to go past the soft eggs with toast, served in a novelty double-headed cup. A perfectly cooked and coddled egg is the epitome of nursery comfort. Yet when you're not eating breakfast in such perfectly adult surroundings, you might crave something more refined than fingers of toast for dunking in your gooey yolk. To me there is no finer implement than a spear of steamed asparagus. Season it and the egg well with a little salt and black pepper. If you want a bit more protein, encircle your trimmed green stems in prosciutto. When I want a touch of elegance in my morning and I can't make it to the hushed marble dining rooms at 160 Piccadilly, this is exactly what I turn to. Now if only I could get hold of a double-headed cup.

2 eggs at room temperature
8 asparagus spears, trimmed
8 strips of prosciutto or jamón, or thin-cut leg ham (optional)
olive oil
sea salt and freshly ground black pepper

Bring a saucepan of water to a rolling boil. Submerge the eggs and boil for 5 minutes and 15 seconds.

While the eggs are cooking, steam the asparagus in a steamer basket above the eggs until they are soft—around 3 minutes.

For a little bit of extra flavor, wrap each asparagus spear in the prosciutto or jamón. Drizzle with olive oil and season with a little salt and pepper.

Carefully cut the top off each egg and dip the asparagus spears into the yolk before eating the remaining white with a small spoon.

SMOKED PAPRIKA CHIA FRITTATAS

Makes 8 mini frittatas, or serves 2 to 3

Breakfast in Barcelona: the gentle sog of pan con tomate—ripe tomatoes ground into griddled white bread, drizzled with olive oil, and seasoned with salt and occasionally a sprinkle of smoked paprika. Add a curl of cured pork and a cortado coffee and a great day is made. Here we take the same flavors and turn them into something a little more sustaining for life back at home. These mini-frittatas are a fistful of protein; from the eggs, to the surprising bulk of plumped chia seeds to the collar of crisp bacon (or jamón). Make them in a nonstick muffin pan and serve them with some arugula and lemon for a swift breakfast. Or stuff a couple in a Tupperware and tote it to work while you dream about the next chance you'll have to get away.

8 strips of bacon or jamón, cut in half crosswise
7 ounces cherry tomatoes
1 garlic clove
1 tablespoon smoked paprika
½ cup chia seeds
4 eggs, lightly beaten
1 teaspoon sea salt

To serve
arugula and lemon wedges

Equipment
1 x 12-cup nonstick muffin pan, greased (if your pan is not nonstick, line the bottom of each cup with a round of parchment paper)

Preheat the oven to 350°F.

Line the inside of 8 muffin-pan cups with 2 half-strips of bacon, overlapping them to ensure that the whole perimeter is covered.

Use a stick blender or food processor to blend together the cherry tomatoes, garlic, and paprika until smooth. Stir together with the chia seeds, eggs, and salt.

Pour the batter into the bacon-lined muffin-pan cups.

Bake the frittatas in the preheated oven for 30 minutes or until the bacon is brown, the frittatas are puffed, and the tops are firm to the touch.

Serve with arugula and a wedge of lemon to squeeze over the frittatas.

FETA, MINT, LENTIL, AND PISTACHIO OMELETS

Serves 2

Lentils and eggs are the suggested power-breakfast of many slow-carb regimes. Here's a way to turn what can be a motley mess on a plate—the sort of thing that a college boy will shovel in his mouth before hitting a weights room that smells of Tuesday's socks—into a meal you can be proud of.

5 tablespoons olive oil
1 x 14-ounce can of brown lentils, rinsed and drained
2 large handfuls of baby spinach
1 teaspoon sea salt
⅓ cup crumbled Persian (marinated) feta
6 eggs
4 tablespoons fresh mint leaves, roughly torn
2 tablespoons pistachios, toasted
freshly ground black pepper

To serve
lemon wedges and chili sauce

Place 1 tablespoon of the olive oil in a nonstick skillet and add the lentils, spinach, and salt. Stir to warm the ingredients through and wilt the spinach. Season with pepper and transfer the contents of the pan to a plate. Crumble the Persian feta over the top of the lentils and set aside while you make your omelets.

Whisk the eggs together in a bowl. Heat 2 tablespoons of the olive oil in the skillet and add half of the egg mixture, swirling the pan to coat the bottom. Cook for 2 minutes or until the top of the omelet is almost set and the base is golden.

Spoon half of the lentil mixture over the half of the omelet that's furthest away from you. Use firm shakes of the pan to jerk the nearest edge of the omelet up the lip of the pan. Use a spatula to fold the nearest half over the filling to enclose it. Slide the omelet onto a plate and scatter with half of the mint leaves and pistachios. Serve with a wedge of lemon and some chili sauce. Repeat with the remaining oil, eggs, and lentil mixture to make a second omelet and garnish with the remaining mint and pistachios.

CHIA BIRCHER MUESLI

Makes 2 to 4 breakfast portions depending on
what you want to have it with and how hungry
you are first thing in the morning

My previous experience with chia was via an allergy-safe pet, shorn with child-friendly scissors. These days it's a new "wonderfood." It's supposedly got more omega-3 than salmon and it's packed full of protein. I've found when dry that it can get stuck in your molars in a way that you thought only a strawberry seed could. But saturate the seeds in a little liquid and they swell up like cheerful orbs of freckled tapioca.

There are very few things that make me happier in the morning than knowing that breakfast is ready-cued in the refrigerator—which is how this muesli substitute was born. To these friendly seeds I add ground flaxseed, yogurt, milk, and a few stray berries for a little fruitiness and flavor. They all hang out together in the refrigerator overnight and meld into a silky, bircher-esque mass. What you then have is a quick but slow (carb) breakfast option that doesn't involve lentils, bacon, or eggs.

I'll sometimes top a portion with a few extra toasted nuts, berries, or seeds—and for the full, more traditional bircher experience, I'll add in a grated apple, skin and all. But most often it's just eaten as is, swiftly out of a bowl, while I wait for the kettle to boil and a good day to roll.

½ cup chia seeds
½ cup rolled oats
1⅔ cups plain yogurt (sheep, goat, soy, or whatever takes
  your fancy)
⅓ cup ground flaxseed (though feel free to substitute with
  bran or oats if you want some more slow-release carbs)
2 handfuls of berries, smooshed with a fork (fresh or frozen)
scant 1½ cups milk

Optional extras
Grated apple, or bran or ground almonds (in which case,
  add the same quantity of yogurt or milk, so it doesn't
  all become too dry); a handful of diced dried pear and
  some chopped Brazil nuts or almonds; fresh berries
  or ½ passionfruit

Equipment
Large tupperware of at least 1-quart capacity

Mix the chia seeds, oats, and yogurt together well to incorporate.

Add the flaxseed, smooshed berries, and milk. Stir very well to prevent globby masses of chia forming in the corners.

Place in the refrigerator for at least 2 hours to soak and incorporate, or overnight.

Stir well once more before serving. Eat on its own, or with some additional fruit, yogurt, and seeds for extra flavor and crunch.

CHAI AND APRICOT QUINOA PORRIDGE

Serves 2

A cup of tea and a bowl of oatmeal—this is how most good mornings should commence. Yet there's no reason why they shouldn't be melded together. And oatmeal need not just be the domain of oats. Quinoa flakes are a novel addition to your pantry (and often stocked in supermarkets, or your local healthfood store). They swell and plump up just like the warming cereals your Nan used to make you on frosty mornings. They're also ripe for adopting other flavors while they cook. This version uses the warmth of chai tea bags with the zip of dried apricots and hazelnuts, though you could just as easily employ Earl Grey or Darjeeling with some dates or prunes. With a small amount of dried fruit or a swirl of jam, some yogurt, and some nuts for crunch, you'll be set for the day.

generous 1 cup milk
generous 1 cup boiling water
2 chai tea bags
generous ½ cup rolled quinoa flakes
3 tablespoons chopped dried apricots or 2 tablespoons apricot jam
3 tablespoons chopped hazelnuts
2 tablespoons plain yogurt, to serve

Bring the milk and water to a simmer in a saucepan. Add the tea bags and let steep for 5 minutes.

Discard the tea bags, then add the quinoa flakes and half of the dried apricots to the liquid. Bring to a boil, then reduce to a simmer and cover. Cook for 10 minutes or until the quinoa is soft and most of the liquid has been absorbed.

Remove from the heat and portion into bowls. Top with the remaining dried apricots (or apricot jam), hazelnuts, and yogurt.

TIP: *Other good combinations to try along with chai are a lick of fig and ginger jam with pistachios, black currant jam with slivered almonds, or some mashed banana with diced Brazil nuts.*

SOFT EGGS WITH
SMOKY BAKED BEANS

Serves 4

Proper, satisfying baked beans cry out for the aroma of a fire. They should be crafted in battered metal pots over coals, combining pork, beans, and a vista that can make you swoon a little. If you can't make it to the great outdoors (or have an innate aversion to the possibility of having ants crawl up your legs while you cook), you can always ape the mystical aroma of fire with a few drops of liquid smoke (available from many gourmet food stores). Shhh, I won't tell if you don't.

For a life-affirming feast all you need are a few soft eggs, a mound of beans, and a strong cup of coffee to the side. The yolks will bleed like a sunrise and the caffeine will give you a proper kick along for whatever you've got planned—even if it's just an afternoon on the couch watching Brokeback Mountain *one more time.*

(If you are planning on making these while out on an intrepid adventure, you can always mix all of the spices, dry ingredients, and sauces together into a slurry at home and tote it along in a glass jar.)

1 tablespoon olive oil
4 ounces bacon, finely diced
2 pork or beef sausages, skin removed and contents rumpled
1 red onion, peeled and cut into slim half-moons
3 garlic cloves, thinly sliced or grated
2 x 14-ounce cans of chopped tomatoes
1 tablespoon Worcestershire sauce
2 tablespoons tomato paste
2 tablespoons dark brown sugar
1 tablespoon apple cider vinegar
1 tablespoon Dijon mustard
1 x 14-ounce can of borlotti beans, rinsed
1 x 14-ounce can of lima or cannellini beans, rinsed
3½ ounces cherry tomatoes
1 teaspoon sea salt
1 teaspoon liquid smoke (optional)
1 tablespoon baking soda
4 eggs at room temperature (older eggs are better)
2 tablespoons fresh flat-leaf parsley leaves, roughly chopped

Put the olive oil, bacon, and sausage meat in a heavy-bottom saucepan or Dutch oven over medium heat. Sauté for 3 minutes or until the bacon has started to gain some color.

Add the onion and garlic and sauté for 5 to 7 minutes until they have begun to soften. Add the chopped tomatoes, Worcestershire sauce, tomato paste, sugar, vinegar, and mustard and bring to a simmer, uncovered.

Add the beans and tomatoes and cook, stirring occasionally, for 15 minutes or until the sauce has reduced, is thick, and is clinging to the beans. Taste and season with the salt to bring the flavors together, and the liquid smoke if you fancy a faux outdoorsy twist.

To cook the eggs, bring a saucepan of water to a rolling boil. Add the baking soda and eggs to the boiling water. Boil the eggs for 5 minutes. Remove them from the pan and run them briefly under cold water. Gently tap the shells against a hard surface and peel them, being careful not to puncture the yolk. Place the peeled eggs in a bowl of warm water until ready to serve.

Serve the beans in bowls with the eggs nestled on top and sprinkled with the parsley. Let the yolk seep into the beans while eating.

TIP: *When boiling the eggs, adding the baking soda to the water helps encourage the whites to shirk away from the shells, making them exponentially easier to peel.*

MEXICAN BAKED EGGS

Serves 4 to 6

Everyone needs a few self-sufficient breakfast recipes. The sort of thing that you can pull together when you're feeling a touch dusty, perhaps from the pleasures of a few too many margaritas the night prior. Baked eggs are a savior. There's no need to mess about with poaching or scrambling to order—just crack a few eggs over a base of spiced black beans and plop them in the oven while you go about organizing juices and caffeine. These ones have a south-of-the-border accent. Serve them with a good thwack of guacamole and some hot sauce and you've got a breakfast that can pull anyone back from the brink, no matter how many shots of Patrón you sipped.

2 red bell peppers, halved and seeded
9 ounces cherry tomatoes, halved
1 tablespoon olive oil, plus extra if needed
2 ounces chorizo, diced (optional)
1 red onion, peeled and diced
1 small chili, diced (and seeded if you don't like things
   too hot)
1 tablespoon ground cumin
½ tablespoon ground coriander
1 pinch of crushed red pepper flakes
1 large handful of fresh cilantro, stems finely chopped
   and leaves set aside
2 x 14-ounce cans of black beans, rinsed
¼ ounce dark chocolate (minimum 70% cocoa solids)
1 teaspoon chipotle purée or ½ teaspoon ground chipotle
   (optional)
4 eggs
4 teaspoons Greek yogurt
sea salt and freshly ground black pepper

Guacamole
2 ripe avocados, pitted and peeled
squeeze of lemon or lime juice
chili sauce (optional)

Equipment
4–6 ramekins or small oven-proof bowls

Preheat the oven to 300°F.

Drizzle the bell peppers and tomatoes with the olive oil and place in the preheated oven to roast for 45 minutes or until lightly blistered. (You can do this the night before if you prefer, or substitute with roasted peppers from a jar, in which case just throw the fresh tomatoes in when you add the beans.)

Place the diced chorizo in a heavy-bottom saucepan or Dutch oven over medium heat. Sauté it until it starts to leach crimson oil. If it is a drier chorizo, you may want to add 1–2 tablespoons olive oil to the pan, then throw in the onion, fresh chili, cumin, coriander, red pepper flakes, and cilantro stems.

Sauté for 5 to 7 minutes or until the onion has softened. Add the black beans, chocolate, and chipotle, if using, and stir to combine.

Take the roasted peppers out of the oven and let them cool just until you can handle them without burning yourself. Raise the oven temperature to 350°F.

Slice the bell peppers and add them, along with the roasted tomatoes and the oil they cooked in, to the pan with the beans. Stir to combine. Taste and adjust the seasoning with salt and pepper and more chili if you want.

Place 2–3 tablespoons of the bean mixture in the bottom and up the sides of each ramekin, creating a well in the center. Ensure there's at least ¾ inch clear at the top for your egg. Place the ramekins on a baking sheet.

Gently crack an egg into each ramekin, taking care not to puncture the yolk. Float a teaspoon of Greek yogurt over the top of the yolk. You can leave your eggs like this until you're ready to eat.

When your guests have arrived and just before you're ready to eat, put the ramekins in the oven and bake them for 10 to 12 minutes or until the whites are solid but the yolks are still a little runny.

While they're baking, make a quick guacamole by mashing the avocado with the cilantro, a squeeze of citrus, and a little chili sauce, if you like. Serve the baked eggs with the guacamole.

TIP: *This will leave you with a little extra beans. They're delicious as a warm salad later on.*

SOCCA WITH SMOKED SALMON AND WHIPPED CURDS

Makes 10 to 12 pancakes depending
on the size of your pan, or serves 4

Introducing socca, the sturdy chickpea flour pancakes that are one of the favored street foods of Nice. They're burnished and have the rough texture of burlap bags. Their taste is nutty and there's a satisfying mix of crisp edges and pliant pockets of batter. They're best served with a bit of rosemary, olive oil, and salt while you sip pink wine and play a novel game of hypothesizing which super-yacht you'd buy if you stumbled across a cool ten million dollars.

They're delightful at the cusp of a day, but they'd also make a lovely snack at the close with a pile of marinated olives and some goat curd and chunks of fennel on the side.

scant 3 cups chickpea (besan or gram) flour, sifted
½ cup olive oil
3½ cups lukewarm water
1 teaspoon ground cumin, to add a slightly smoky flavor
  (optional)
sea salt, to balance any bitterness in the chickpea flour
butter or olive oil, to grease
1½ cups cottage cheese
2 teaspoons apple cider vinegar
1 teaspoon honey or rice malt syrup
2 scallions, diced
7 ounces smoked salmon

Equipment
a nonstick skillet or pancake pan is vital

Combine the chickpea flour and olive oil, whisking them together with a balloon whisk. Whisk in the water and cumin, if using, and let rest for 30 minutes. Taste a little of the batter and add salt if it seems bitter.

Heat a nonstick skillet or pancake pan over medium heat and swipe with butter or olive oil. Pour in just enough batter to coat the bottom and swirl around. Cook until you can easily lift the pancake from the bottom of the pan. Use a large spatula to gently flip the pancake over, then cook the other side until browned. Keep it warm in a low oven while you make the remaining pancakes.

Blend the cottage cheese with the vinegar and honey until smooth.

To assemble, stack the pancakes with the cottage cheese and scallions. Top with smoked salmon.

TIP: *Be sure to taste the batter before you start—if you're using unroasted chickpea flour it can have a bitter taste. This can be mitigated by adding more salt. Also be sure to whisk the batter well before starting, as the flour sediment can sink to the bottom of the bowl. The first pancake may be no good. This happens. Be sure that your pan is well greased before starting.*

TIP: *You can usually find chickpea flour (sometimes known as besan or gram) in the Indian section of a grocery store.*

BLACK FOREST SLOW GRANOLA PARFAITS

Serves 4 to 6

This granola takes the alchemic combination of cocoa, cherries, and dairy and puts them to a more restrained use than in a slice of torte. There are a few secrets to golden granola; chief among them is using egg whites to help the grains gather into plump clumps. Beyond that there's olive oil for superior crunch, ensuring there's a good mix of grains, and only adding the dried fruit after the grains have been baked. Be sure to add whatever nuts are your favorite— mine are macadamias and hazelnuts—but almonds and walnuts would also be grand. All that's left is to add a pinch or two of salt to curb the sweetness and keep this giddily delicious combination at the adult end of the spectrum. You may be eating cocoa for breakfast, but this layered treat is a long way from the domain of snap, crackle, and pop.

1 cup rolled oats
⅓ cup ground flaxseed
⅓ cup dry unsweetened coconut
scant ½ cup hazelnuts, roughly chopped
scant ¼ cup macadamias, roughly chopped
2 teaspoons ground cinnamon
3 tablespoons unsweetened cocoa
1–2 teaspoons sea salt flakes
4 tablespoons olive oil
¼ cup rice malt syrup or pure maple syrup
1 egg white, beaten until foamy
5 ounces dried cherries

To serve
4 cups Greek yogurt and 7 ounces drained
   Morello cherries

Equipment
baking sheet lined with parchment paper

Preheat the oven to 285°F.

Mix all the dry ingredients together (except the dried cherries) in a big bowl.

Heat the olive oil and syrup together in a small pan until bubbling and pour the mixture over the dry ingredients in the bowl.

Mix everything together until well coated, then fold through the beaten egg white. Pour it onto the lined baking sheet and bake in the preheated oven for 45 minutes. Turn the granola over with a spoon, return it to the oven, and bake for another 25 minutes or until the nuts are crunchy. Let it cool for 15 minutes, then break up the clumps.

Combine the granola clumps with the dried cherries. Either put the granola in an airtight container to keep, or assemble the parfaits.

To assemble the parfaits, take 4 glasses or tumblers and layer them with yogurt, cherries, and granola, then more yogurt, cherries, and granola. Serve immediately.

Drinks and nibbles can be a slightly sticky time if you're trying to avoid the starches. The reason? Bread. It's the standard fodder we lean on to help fill a hole before a meal commences; whether grissini with olives, pita with dips, or charred bruschetta. Yet as soon as you start thinking outside the box you'll discover a wide array of alternative snacks and appetizers.

Whether it's a whole steamed artichoke which starts as a table decoration before being slowly dismantled petal by petal and dragged through aïoli, or the perfect recipe for kale chips (which really became that popular for a reason), you'll be set.

As for us, if it's just a Friday night at home celebrating the close of a long week The Hungry One will usually open the canisters of five-spice soy almonds and spiced chickpea bombs which live in the pantry while he cracks through a beer. If we've got guests gathered around the barbecue then it's roasted tomato and halloumi skewers and some cannellini bean dip with crudités. And if I'm feeling cheeky and festive, then it's hard to walk away from a platter of pigs in kimchee blankets. As long as there's a mix of bright spice and crunch (and something cheerful in a glass to go with it), we're happy.

LIGHT SNACKS TO SERVE WITH DRINKS

CANNELLINI BEAN, PARMESAN, AND ARTICHOKE DIP WITH CRUDITÉS

Makes 1.5 cups, or serves 4 to 6

I can usually be trusted to behave at a party. I'll bring something nice to eat, a chilled bottle of wine, and a pair of shoes that says "I care enough to not wear sneakers to your soirée, but I can still stand in these for an hour." I can be perfectly social, except when this dip is on offer. Because then there's every chance I'm going to take a small bowl and run away to a quiet corner and eat it all. There's something about the unsung, holy trinity of artichokes, Parmesan, and pale beans. It's a communion of earth and brightness, the Parmesan adds richness, the beans offer a mild sweetness, and the artichokes contribute a curious twang of acid. I've leaned on this trio before in a simple braise with chicken thighs, leeks, stock, and baby spinach but I think it's here, in a dip made solid with white beans and served with crisp crudités, that their charms really come to the fore.

1 x 10-ounce jar of marinated artichoke hearts (6–7 ounces drained artichokes, but reserve the marinade)
1 x 14-ounce can of cannellini beans, rinsed
1 tablespoon fresh flat-leaf parsley leaves, roughly chopped
¼ cup grated Parmesan
grated zest and juice of ½ lemon
½ teaspoon freshly ground black pepper

To serve
1 bunch of baby carrots, scrubbed clean; 1 fennel bulb, bottom trimmed, and cut into slim wedges; cherry tomatoes, on skewers

Spoon 2 tablespoons of the artichoke heart marinade into a blender. Drain the rest.

Add the artichoke hearts, cannellini beans, parsley, Parmesan, lemon zest and juice, and the black pepper. Blend until smooth. If it is too thick, add 1–2 tablespoons of hot water or olive oil to create a more pliable, dip-like consistency.

Serve the dip with the crudités.

RADISHES WITH BUTTER AND TRUFFLE SALT

Serves 4

Sometimes I like to pretend I'm in France—or that I'm much more soignée than I am. One way is to pull out a Breton striped shirt and a silk scarf. The other way is to serve this dish to guests. Radishes with butter and salt are a classic bistro appetizer, often paired with a crusty baguette. Yet the crunch of the radishes, particularly if they've been perked up in iced water, has little need for a yeasted dough. Instead, try adding the murky flavor of truffle to the combination for a deft bit of distraction. The mushroomy aroma of truffled salt (available from many delis) adds an interesting complexity. If you really want to push the boat out, though, try serving the butter melted with a few slivers of fresh truffle floating and infusing in it.

1 small bunch of radishes (around 8), scrubbed clean and halved
3 tablespoons unsalted butter, at room temperature
1 tablespoon truffle salt

Soak the radishes in iced water for 10 to 15 minutes until they are crisp. Dry well before serving.

Present the radishes on a platter with the softened butter in one dish and the truffle salt in another. Encourage guests to swipe a radish half through the butter and then dip it into the truffle salt. No double dipping, please.

FIVE-SPICE SOY ROASTED ALMONDS

Serves 6 to 8

These are addictive. They're crunchy and salty, sweet and spiced. They remind me of the honey-soy chicken drumsticks my mother used to bake and serve over brown rice on Wednesday nights in 1989. They store perfectly in a Tupperware in the pantry. They pair just as well with a cold ale at 6 p.m. when you walk in the door, as they do with a cup of green tea at 2.30 a.m. when you're starving and desperately trying to finish a presentation. And they're a neat way to add a bit of extra crunch to a simple dinner: whether sautéed greens with a soft cooked egg, soy-marinated flank steak with ribbons of carrot, or even simple baked chicken drumsticks.

1⅔ cups almonds
3 tablespoons light soy sauce
½ tablespoon runny honey or rice malt syrup
2 teaspoons Chinese five-spice powder
sea salt

Equipment
rimmed baking sheet lined with parchment paper

Preheat the oven to 300°F.

Spread the almonds in a single layer on the lined baking sheet and bake them in the preheated oven for about 10 minutes, or until they smell nutty. Leave the oven on.

Transfer them to a heatproof bowl. Mix together the soy, honey, and five-spice powder in a small bowl, then pour it over the almonds. Stir to coat them well.

Transfer the almonds back to the baking sheet in a single layer. Bake them again, stirring occasionally, for 15 to 18 minutes until they are dry and browned.

Taste and season with salt if needed. Serve them warm, or let them cool completely before storing in an airtight container.

KALE CHIPS WITH LEMON

Serves 2 to 4, with drinks

I wanted to hate kale chips. I wanted to shun them the way I do event television and wedge sneakers. They flamed into the zeitgeist too quickly; they were too faddish; they came from nowhere—like an edible meme—and suddenly they were everywhere, haunting every corner of the internet and wholefood store. But here's the problem: they're very good. They have a pleasant crackle and an elegant texture. And surprisingly for a roasted leaf, they also proved an excellent vehicle for other flavors. You could try them with smoked paprika sprinkled over the top. Cayenne or Sichuan pepper would also be fun. But lemon zest makes them really shine—as though the last thing these chips needed was anything to draw more of a spotlight onto them.

small bunch of kale, about 7 ounces, cleaned and
   dried thoroughly
2 tablespoons olive oil
grated zest of 1 lemon
sea salt

Equipment
baking sheet lined with parchment paper

Preheat the oven to 350°F.

Pull the tendrils of the kale away from the hard stems and discard the stems. Gently tear the tendrils into pieces about the size of a Pringle.

Scatter the kale in a single layer over the lined baking sheet. You may have to do this in batches. Drizzle the kale with the olive oil, and sprinkle with the lemon zest and some salt, to taste.

Roast the kale in the preheated oven until mostly crisp—10 to 13 minutes. If it's browning too much, turn some of the leaves over. A word of caution: if you bake them to the browner edge, they will taste more roasted and a little more bitter.

Let the kale cool completely before storing in an airtight container.

PADRÓN PEPPERS WITH JAMÓN SALT

Serves 4

It just makes sense that these two things should be joined together. It's a rare occasion that a bowl of blistered pimientos de Padrón isn't followed by a platter of cured meats. These small peppers hailing from northwest Spain are both a grand appetizer and a gamble—anywhere between five and twenty percent of them will be blazingly hot. You can try and guess which ones they will be, but really, the best way is to suck them and see.

For those who don't fancy cured meat in their salt, feel free to season the peppers liberally with just Maldon salt flakes, or the salt flakes combined with some smoked paprika or lemon zest.

¾ ounce jamón
1 tablespoon sea salt flakes
1 tablespoon olive oil
11 ounces padrón peppers

To make the jamón salt, put the jamón in a saucepan and cook it over medium heat until it is crisp. Remove it from the pan and let it cool.

Put the cooled jamón in a food processor and blitz to make fine crumbs, then mix them with the salt flakes. Alternatively, grind it with the salt using a mortar and pestle. Set aside.

To cook the peppers, heat the olive oil in a deep skillet over medium heat. When the oil is simmering, add the peppers.

Cook and stir the peppers until their skins are brown and blistered. Careful—they may spit.

Remove the peppers from the pan, place on a plate, and sprinkle with the jamón salt, to taste.

EDAMAME WITH BROWN RICE TEA SALT

Serves 4

I doubt at this stage whether anyone needs any instruction on how to eat edamame, those immature soybeans in pods that have become a ubiquitous appetizer at most Japanese restaurants and sushi-go-arounds. But just in case, here's a hint. Don't eat the case. It's leathery and tough and as unpalatable as can be. And you'll look a little foolish. Instead, transfer the pod directly to your mouth and use your teeth to extract each bean. Lightly steamed or boiled, these beans are naturally sweet—a little sprinkling of salt is what really makes them sing. And for a nifty twist, try muddling your salt with some brown rice tea. It offers a smoky depth that makes for a compelling slow-carb snack.

1 tablespoon sea salt flakes
1 tea bag of Japanese brown rice tea (genmaicha), or a green tea bag
1 pound 2 ounces frozen edamame in their pods

Mix together the sea salt and the contents of the brown rice tea bag.

Bring a saucepan of water to a boil. Add the frozen edamame and cook for about 4 minutes, or until the pods turn bright green and are heated through. Drain them and transfer them to a large bowl. Toss them with the brown rice tea salt and serve them with a bowl to the side for the empty casings.

PIGS IN KIMCHEE BLANKETS

Serves 4

You might not think that spicy, fermented Korean cabbage, tiny sausages, a sweet glaze, and a downy tuft of Parmesan cheese would be friends. You may, in fact, think that I'm mad for clumping them together on a toothpick. But please, trust me here. Pigs in blankets on their own—that cocktail staple and barnyard coupling of sausage with a coat of cured pig or pastry—is too much. Too much meat, too much fat; too one-dimensional in its notes of squish and salt. Here it gets taken out for a spin by two exotic friends, and is all the better for it. The kimchee adds a kooky layer of acidity and spice. The rice-malt glaze gives a sweet shine, and the Parmesan provides the final twirl of complexity—an umami roundness that takes it to the next level completely. Essentially, what you're looking at are the core ingredients in the most hipster of hotdogs, bar the bread, which I think most of us will agree can be the most boring bit of all.

8 slices of bacon, trimmed to 4 inches long and 1¼ inches wide
5½ ounces kimchee
8 good-quality chipolata sausages
1½ tablespoons rice malt syrup or pure maple syrup
¼ cup finely grated Parmesan

Equipment
8 toothpicks
baking sheet lined with parchment paper

Preheat the oven to 350°F.

Lay out the slices of bacon and cover each one with a dollop of kimchee.

Swaddle each raw chipolata in kimchee and bacon, with the bacon outermost. Thread a toothpick through the bacon to fasten it closed and pin it to the sausage.

Arrange the blanketed pigs on the lined baking sheet and brush them with the syrup. Bake them in the preheated oven for 30 to 35 minutes, until the bacon is brown and the sausages are piping hot.

Sprinkle the Parmesan over the pigs in blankets just before serving with napkins—and possibly a cold ale or two.

QUINOA AND ZUCCHINI FRITTERS WITH STRAINED YOGURT

Makes 12 to 14

These natty vegetarian and gluten-free fritters are as happy on a tray with drinks while you watch the sun slip down with a crowd of six, as they are at a breakfast for two. There are so many winning aspects—from the earthiness of the grated zucchini to the sparkle of salt from the olive tapenade. Then there are the quinoa flakes which offer both protein and the body to bind them together. They're delightful with strained yogurt or feta cheese crumbled over the top but they are also outstanding with some smoked salmon or a poached egg if what you're really after is a substantial supper for one.

2 medium zucchini, grated
½ cup rolled quinoa flakes
¼ cup milk
4 tablespoons olive tapenade
a pinch of crushed red pepper flakes (optional)
2 eggs, lightly beaten
15 fresh mint leaves, very finely chopped
handful of fresh flat-leaf parsley leaves, very finely chopped
1 scallion, diced
1 teaspoon sea salt
4 tablespoons olive oil

To serve
1¼ cups Greek yogurt and 1 teaspoon sea salt; chili sauce
  (optional)

Stir together the zucchini, quinoa flakes, milk, tapenade, red pepper flakes, eggs, mint, parsley, scallion, and salt until well combined.

Put half of the olive oil in a nonstick skillet. Drop in 1 tablespoon of batter per fritter and fry until golden on the bottom. You can probably do 3–4 at a time. Use a spatula to gently flip the fritters over, then cook the other sides until the outsides are crisp and the fritters hold together. Keep them warm in a low oven while you make the remaining fritters using the remaining oil to grease the pan.

To serve, season the yogurt with the salt and dollop on the fritters, perhaps with some chili sauce on the side.

TIP: *These can be made ahead and frozen in Tupperware between slips of parchment paper; just reinvigorate them in the oven, a pan, or toasted sandwich press.*

ROASTED AND FRESH TOMATO SKEWERS WITH MINT AND HALLOUMI

Serves 4

Snacks on toothpicks have a certain retro whimsy. These appetizers follow that lead, but with a modern twist; no cheddar or pineapple chunks here, thanks. Instead you'll find that tomato with mint and sheep's milk cheese form a cracking combination—sweet and acidic, fresh and milky all at once. Halloumi can occasionally have the texture of a kitchen sponge, particularly when it's overcooked. The key is to broil it over a blazing surface just long enough for the outside to caramelize and the interior to relax. Check if your surface is hot enough by placing half a lemon, cut side down, on it. If it sizzles on contact, you're right to start cooking. Once the skewers are done, you'll have a ready-made dressing in the blistered lemons: winner.

16 cherry tomatoes, halved
3 tablespoons olive oil
a pinch of sea salt
1 lemon, halved
6½ ounces halloumi cheese, cut horizontally into
  ½-inch thick slices
16 fresh mint leaves

Equipment
16 toothpicks

Preheat the oven to 350°F.

Place half of the tomatoes, cut side up, in a baking dish and drizzle with 1 tablespoon of the olive oil, and the salt. Bake them in the preheated oven for 20 minutes, or until the tops have started to blister and soften.

Five minutes before the tomatoes are ready, heat the remaining olive oil in a nonstick skillet over medium heat. Test when the pan is hot enough by placing the 2 lemon halves, cut side down, in the pan. When they sizzle, it's time to add the halloumi slices. Leave the lemon where it is and add the halloumi. Fry it for 2 to 3 minutes on each side until it has developed a mottled brown tan. The lemon should also have caramelized, creating an instant dressing for the halloumi.

Drain the halloumi on paper towels, then cut each slice into 8 pieces the size of a postage stamp. Skewer onto a toothpick a piece of halloumi, a roasted tomato half, a mint leaf, and a fresh tomato half. Serve them hot, with the blistered lemon halves on the side to squeeze over.

ARTICHOKES WITH RED-EYE AÏOLI

Serves 4

A whole artichoke is hospitality in a nutshell, clubbing together in one neat package both your centerpiece and appetizer. Next time you have guests over in spring—when artichokes are at their best—consider steaming a whole beauty and allow your guests to collectively pull off frond after frond, scraping the curved bases lazily against their lower teeth to extract every scratch of flesh. You could join it with a simple vinaigrette of olive oil, Dijon mustard, and red wine vinegar for dipping. Or you could take a cue from the American South, a place that has perfected the art of hosting. This red-eye aïoli takes its inspiration from the classic southern red-eye gravy, which uses the depth and smokiness of coffee to counterpoint the saltiness of ham and bacon. It's a notion that applies just as well to a steamed and seasoned artichoke. Muddle the red eye aïoli ("red eye-oli") together, put it on a platter with the artichoke, and don't forget a bowl for the discarded leaves. If, despite all your best efforts to make things convivial, conversation flails, rest assured you can always play the game of "guess the secret ingredient in the sauce."

1 large artichoke
1 fresh or dried bay leaf
½ lemon
hot water, to cover

Red-eye aïoli
1 egg yolk
scant ½ cup sunflower oil
1 small garlic clove, grated
2 teaspoons espresso at room temperature
a good pinch of sea salt

To cook the artichoke, first cut off the top ¾ inch from where the leaves are tightly bunched, like a bud. Also trim the stem to just ¾ inch in length. If the sharp points of the remaining leaves are particularly spiky, you can trim them too (or just be careful while you eat it not to stab yourself).

Put the artichoke in a large pot and pour in enough hot water to come three-quarters of the way up the artichoke. Add the bay leaf and lemon and clamp a lid on the pot. Bring the water to a boil, then lower the heat so that the water is just simmering. Simmer for 25 to 45 minutes or until you can easily pull the outer leaves off.

To make the aïoli, place a wet dish towel under a clean bowl (this will help make the bowl more stable). Whisk the egg yolk for 30 seconds to help get some air into it.

Very slowly trickle a small amount of oil down the side of the bowl. Whisk until it has emulsified with the egg yolk. Do this again. And again and again. Do not pour freely until you have a good, thick, and glossy-looking mayonnaise. If you've split the mayonnaise and it won't take the oil, don't throw out what you have. Just get a fresh bowl and crack another egg yolk into it. Now trickle the oil/egg mixture in, bit by bit. When that has turned into a mayonnaise, add the remaining oil.

When you're satisfied with your mayonnaise, turn it into the red-eye aïoli by adding the garlic and coffee. Stir, then season generously with salt. Taste. If you think it needs more, add more salt to help balance the flavors.

Serve the warm artichoke in the middle of the table and let people pull off leaves and dunk the bases in the aïoli.

SPICED CHICKPEA BOMBS

Serves 4

Who knew that chickpeas, when roasted in a little bit of olive oil, turn into crisp balls which shatter like your favorite party mix? If you did—well done. If not, do try these. They're simple to make and the perfect thing to lay out with a stiff drink at the end of a long day. I like them with a bit of a spicy kick but if you prefer a milder flavor, omit the cayenne and perhaps add some ground cinnamon or ginger for a more romantic lilt. The best thing about these is that I bet all the ingredients are in your pantry, most of the time. So if you get stuck having people over and need something nifty to serve, a novel thing to pick at is only 30 minutes away.

1 x 14-ounce can of chickpeas, rinsed and dried thoroughly
3 tablespoons olive oil
½–1 tablespoon ground cayenne pepper (depending on how spicy you like things)
1 tablespoon ground cumin
1 tablespoon ground coriander
1 teaspoon sea salt

Equipment
baking sheet lined with parchment paper

Preheat the oven to 375°F.

Scatter the chickpeas over the lined baking sheet in a single layer.

Mix together the olive oil, cayenne, cumin, and coriander in a small bowl, then scatter it over the chickpeas. Stir to coat them well.

Bake the chickpeas in the preheated oven for about 20 minutes.

Shake the sheet a little to move the chickpeas around and allow all the surfaces to get some heat from the oven. Return the sheet to the oven for another 15 minutes until the chickpeas are crispy.

Remove the sheet from the oven, sprinkle the chickpeas with the salt, and let them cool before eating or storing them in an airtight container.

ZUCCHINI FRITES

Serves 4 to 6

You can get lofty and call them frites but really, fries are fries. They're slivers of vegetable, cooked in oil until crisp, then seasoned and consumed—often by the fistful. They're what you want as a side to a steak. They're perfect dabbed in mustard alongside a roast chicken. And they shouldn't be constrained to starches. These frites are a little lighter than their potato-based cousin. Zucchini offer a yielding center while the chickpea flour and soda water in the batter crisp up beautifully. Granted, these are not everyday food, so treat them as an exotic visitor and dust them in za'atar, a blend of oregano, thyme, and sesame. Spritz them with lemon. Maybe dip them in yogurt and sesame seed paste. Then savor every hot, salty bite.

scant ⅔ cup chickpea (besan or gram) flour
½ teaspoon baking powder
½ teaspoon freshly ground black pepper
½ tablespoon ground coriander
1 egg yolk, whisked
½ tablespoon vegetable oil
½ cup soda water
3 medium zucchini, cut into thin ½-inch sticks
1 tablespoon table salt
generous 2–3 cups vegetable oil, for frying
1½ tablespoons za'atar

Whisk together the flour, baking powder, pepper, and coriander in a large bowl. Drizzle the egg yolk and the ½ tablespoon of oil into the bowl and use a fork to create a craggy dough. Slowly pour in the soda water, whisking continuously until a smooth batter forms. Cover with plastic wrap and chill for at least 1 hour.

When you are ready to fry the frites, heat the oil for frying in a large saucepan until it reaches 375°F on a cooking thermometer. If you don't have a thermometer, the oil is ready when a cube of bread dropped into it browns in 30 seconds.

Take a handful of zucchini sticks, drop them into the batter, and make sure they're well coated. Use tongs to gently lower them into the hot oil and fry them until they're golden—about 4 minutes. Remove them from the oil with a slotted spoon and drain them on paper towels. Let the oil return to 375°F and repeat the process with the remaining sticks and batter.

Sprinkle the frites with the salt and za'atar before serving. If you fancy a condiment, then plain yogurt muddled with some olive oil and lemon juice works well.

There are few things more comforting than a good bowl of soup. I'm not talking about meek broths. I'm talking about chunky, hearty bowls of sustenance. The sort which, while you eat them with a spoon, keeping a fork nearby won't seem like complete folly.

Most of what follows makes a perfect swift lunch; portioned into sandwich bags and frozen, it also makes excellent backup suppers on cold nights when you need to be warmed from the inside out. In winter it's a rare week when there's not a simmering pot of the ultimate ham and lentil soup, or ribollita on the stove. On those steaming summer eves when it's too hot to think let alone cook, I take comfort in knowing that I can have a cooling bowl of white bean, cucumber, mint, and yogurt, or curried chickpea soup in a bowl in less time than it takes to soften an onion. And if I'm feeling poorly, nothing fails to bring me back from the brink like the "all the Nanas' chicken, lemon, egg, and white bean soup," though the quinoa aguadito with its perky strains of cilantro and lime comes a close second.

SOUPS (A DIFFERENT KIND OF LIQUID LUNCH)

ALL THE NANAS' CHICKEN, LEMON, EGG, AND WHITE BEAN SOUP

Serves 2

This soup came to me when I called on the wisdom of all the Nanas I know to bring me back from the brink of a terrible cold. There's chicken stock, poached chicken, carrot, and celery—the necessary base of all restorative soups. There's a slight Asian lilt from the garlic and chili. There are beans for sustenance. And in the spirit of Greek avgolemono the lemon and beaten egg added at the end evolve into a gentle spider web of protein through the bowl. To save this dish just for days when you're poorly, though, would be a waste. It also tastes grand when you're at your best but someone close to you needs a little helping hand.

2 chicken breasts
1 small red chili, seeded and diced
1 carrot, peeled and finely diced
1 rib of celery, finely diced
2¾ cups good-quality chicken stock (homemade is best)
1 x 14-ounce can of white beans, rinsed
2 eggs, beaten
1 lemon, quartered
handful of fresh flat-leaf parsley leaves, chopped
sea salt and freshly ground black pepper

Put the chicken breasts, chili, carrot, and celery in a saucepan with the chicken stock over medium heat. Bring the stock up to a simmer and poach the contents until the chicken is cooked through and shreds easily—about 10 to 15 minutes. Remove the chicken from the pan, shred it with 2 forks and divide it between 2 soup bowls. Set the pan aside with its contents.

Divide the beans between the bowls with the chicken.

Pour the beaten egg into the pan with the simmering chicken stock and vegetables and keep the pan over medium heat, stirring until the egg collects in threads.

Season the soup with salt, pepper, and lemon juice. You want the soup to have personality. Divide the soup between the soup bowls and top with chopped parsley and a lemon wedge.

ULTIMATE HAM
AND LENTIL SOUP

Serves 4 to 6

There is very little that is sexy about lentil soup. Yet like many frumpy things (flight socks, dental floss, flesh-toned underwear, etc.), it's incredibly useful. It makes a sturdy lunch; it freezes beautifully; and it's a soup that actually works for supper. All it needs is a couple of tricks to transform it into a shining staple. Firstly, try to beg off your local deli their jamón or prosciutto ends—they offer a depth of flavor far beyond what you'd get from a ham bone (while also avoiding the unsightly jellification you'll get from hock). The other trick is to include diced nori strips—while there is little that's Japanese about this dish, the seaweed plays in the same umami key as the jamón, melting into the soup and making it earthy, savory, and utterly delicious.

1½ cups green or brown lentils (or a mix of both)
1 tablespoon olive oil
1 onion, peeled and diced
1 carrot, peeled and finely diced
2 fresh or dried bay leaves
11 ounces jamón or prosciutto ends, cut into pieces the size of a matchbox (be sure to trim off any large sections of fat and remove any twine or plastic that's sneakily sticking out)
8 cups vegetable stock
2 tablespoons nori strips

To serve
grated zest and juice of ½ lemon, and olive oil

Soak the lentils in a bowl of cold water for 1 hour, then drain and discard the water.

Add the olive oil to a heavy-bottom saucepan or Dutch oven over medium heat. Add the onion and carrot and sauté for 5 to 7 minutes until softened. Add the lentils, bay leaves, chunky jamón or prosciutto ends, vegetable stock, and nori and bring to a boil.

Reduce the heat and simmer, covered with a lid, for 1 to 2 hours, until the lentils have broken down and the jamón or prosciutto has imparted a savory flavor.

Remove the jamón or prosciutto and bay leaves from the soup and use a balloon whisk to encourage some of the lentils to break down further. Shred the ham with 2 forks if you can and return it to the pan to mix it in. Portion the soup into bowls. Brighten it up with a little lemon zest and juice and a glug of olive oil.

TIP: *The inclusion of the seaweed in this soup helps to mollify the trumpeting potential side effects of a large bowl of beans.*

TURKISH RED LENTIL SOUP

Serves 6

Red lentil soup can rescue you from anything, whether it's a crummy morning marred by parking tickets, or torrential Turkish rain en route to the Aya Sofia just before you discover it's closed for the day. This soup is a balance of excitement and comfort, with the smooth texture of the lentils playing second fiddle to the thrum of cumin and the trilling of sumac, that berry-red and slightly sour spice. This makes a terrific vegetarian supper on its own perhaps with some Swiss chard or kale stirred through at the end. But if you're the sort of person who needs some meat for a meal to feel complete, a few browned lamb meatballs bobbing around in the bottom of the bowl won't go astray.

1½ tablespoons ground cumin
3 tablespoons olive oil
2 red onions, peeled and finely diced
2 garlic cloves, minced or finely diced
2 carrots, peeled and diced
3 tablespoons tomato paste
2½ cups red lentils, washed
1 quart water
sea salt

To serve
3 tablespoons labneh (strained Greek yogurt)
small bunch of fresh mint leaves, torn
3 teaspoons sumac
chili, finely shredded kale, or browned lamb meatballs
  (all optional)

Put the cumin in a heavy-bottom saucepan or Dutch oven over medium heat. Toast for 1 minute or until it smells nutty, then pour in the oil.

Add the onions, garlic, and carrots and sauté for about 5 to 7 minutes until they have softened. Add the tomato paste and stir to combine.

Add the lentils, pour in the water, and bring it to a boil. Once it has boiled, turn the heat down to bring the liquid to a simmer and cover the pan with the lid. Cook for 20 to 25 minutes, until the lentils have broken down, stirring occasionally to prevent anything from catching on the bottom of the pan.

Add ½ tablespoon sea salt, turn off the heat, and leave with the lid on for another 5 to 10 minutes.

Using a stick blender or food processor, blend the soup until smooth. Check the seasoning and add more salt to taste.

Serve the soup with a splash of labneh, fresh mint leaves, and a good sprinkling of sumac. Chili, kale, and meatballs are all optional.

RIBOLLITA

Serves 4 to 6

A true Tuscan ribollita is bulked out with stale bread. This is not that soup. In fact, it's probably a stretch even claiming it a member of its extended family. But whatever its moniker, this is definitely a worthy dish for your winter repertoire. It's rustic and filling with blended beans and tastes surprisingly complex courtesy of the sneaky inclusion of a Parmesan rind in the stock. For a meat-free version, omit the bacon pieces and replace the chicken stock with vegetable. But it's best not to overlook the pesto recipe at the end—it will keep well in the refrigerator covered in some olive oil and elevates this rough and ready stew from a homely dish to something I'd happily serve up to company, any day of the week.

If you are serving it to guests, think about following it up with something equally hearty but slightly more refined, like the Orange, Chocolate, and Hazelnut Puddings on page 170.

1 tablespoon olive oil
3½ ounces small bacon pieces or bacon cut into thin sticks
1 tablespoon fennel seeds
1 red onion, peeled and diced
2 carrots, peeled and diced
½ fennel bulb, diced
3 garlic cloves, peeled and thinly sliced
½–1 teaspoon crushed red pepper flakes
2 x 14-ounce cans of cannellini beans, rinsed
3 cups chicken stock
1 Parmesan rind
7 ounces cavolo nero or kale, leaves and stalks thinly sliced
sea salt and freshly ground black pepper

Arugula, lemon, and walnut pesto
large handful of baby arugula
grated zest of ½ lemon
½ garlic clove
2 tablespoons chopped walnuts
¼ cup grated Parmesan
¼ cup olive oil

Heat the olive oil in a heavy-bottom saucepan or Dutch oven over medium heat. Add the bacon and fennel seeds and sauté until the bacon fat begins to render. Add the onion, carrots, fennel, garlic, and red pepper flakes and sauté over low–medium heat for 10 to 12 minutes until the vegetables have started to soften.

Tip one can of rinsed beans into a food processor with the chicken stock and blitz to a purée. Add the liquid to the pan along with the other can of whole beans and the Parmesan rind. Simmer, covered with the lid, for 30 minutes.

After 30 minutes, add the cavolo nero or kale and simmer, uncovered, for 10 minutes to soften.

To make the arugula, lemon, and walnut pesto, blend all the ingredients together in a food processor until smooth. Taste and season with salt and pepper.

Remove the Parmesan rind from the soup. Portion into bowls and serve with a generous dollop of the pesto on top.

ROAST BLOODY MARY TOMATO SOUP

Serves 4

There are things you miss, both while growing a small person inside of you and in the aftermath of trying to feed them off your own body. For me, Bloody Marys were chief among them. That sprightly combination of tomato juice, vodka, Worcestershire, and Tabasco with a swizzle stick of celery is downright celebratory and a hallmark of a good time on any side of the globe. It was from those unfulfilled cravings that this virgin version was born, substituting the warmth from the booze for some time in the oven. Both the celery and tomatoes become deepened and softened after a spell and the roast garlic adds a surprising sweetness. The white beans are optional, but they do help make it more substantial, without interrupting the flavor profile too much. The only thing to be careful of is the amount of heat you add. The second time I made this I turned up the volume, savoring the burn. Two hours later I fed my six-week-old son. Sometimes a Bloody Mary can keep you up all night for good reasons. This was not one. In the hours that followed, my son fussed and fretted, spilled and complained, until I finally clocked that not everyone likes things to be searingly hot. So learn from my mistakes and proceed with caution; you can always add more spice, but once it's there, it can be rather hard to take it away.

1 whole garlic bulb with the top lopped off
9 ounces celery (or 3 ribs) cut into sticks 2½ inches long (leafy ends set aside for serving)
1¾ pounds (or 10–12) ripe Roma tomatoes, halved lengthwise
4 tablespoons olive oil
2 teaspoons sea salt
1–2 teaspoons crushed red flakes (depending on how hot you like things)
1 x 14-ounce can of white beans, rinsed
2 tablespoons Worcestershire sauce
juice of ½ lemon
½ cup water
Tabasco, to taste

Preheat the oven to 300°F.

Put the garlic, celery, and Roma tomatoes, cut side up, on a rimmed baking sheet. Drizzle with the olive oil and sprinkle with the salt and red pepper flakes. Roast them in the preheated oven for 1½ hours or until the tomatoes have puckered. Let them cool for 5 to 10 minutes.

Squeeze the roasted garlic cloves out of their casings and add them to a food processor or blender with the roasted vegetables and any juices from the baking sheet. Add the beans, Worcestershire, lemon juice, and water and blend until smooth. Taste and season with extra salt, red pepper flakes, or lemon juice, if required.

Serve the soup hot with the celery ends for dipping and Tabasco for those who want an extra kick.

TIP: *If you fancy a bit more protein you can also transform this into a "red eye" with a poached egg floating in the center.*

CHILLED WHITE BEAN, CUCUMBER, MINT, AND YOGURT SOUP

Serves 1 to 2

There are days when it's too hot to think, let alone cook. When those occasions of sweltering summer descend, this what I turn to. It's not quite a gazpacho and it's not quite tzatziki. There's a streak of garlic and lemon for zing, the floral softness of cucumber, the body of white beans, and the lightness of yogurt. If you're after something refined, strain it before serving and take care with the placement of the olives, mint leaves, and pistachios. If you're merely hot and hungry, whizz it until it's as smooth as you think it will go and portion it straight into bowls, leaving the adornments out on the table for everyone to fix themselves.

½ large cucumber
1 x 14-ounce can of white beans, rinsed
grated zest and juice of ½ lemon
1¼ cups Greek yogurt
1 small garlic clove, peeled and grated
handful of fresh mint leaves
1 ice cube
1 tablespoon olive oil, plus extra to drizzle
sea salt and freshly ground black pepper
handful of shelled pistachios
handful of green olives, pitted and sliced
green chili, diced (optional)

Grate the cucumber into a bowl and add the beans, lemon zest and juice, yogurt, garlic, and three-quarters of the mint leaves.

Blitz the ingredients in the bowl with a stick blender or in a food processor until they are all combined and well blended. Add the ice cube and let it melt and chill the soup down.

If you prefer a smoother, more elegant soup, now strain it through a strainer.

Season the soup with salt, pepper, and the olive oil, then portion it into bowls. Top with the remaining mint, the pistachios, and olives and a drizzle more of olive oil, if needed. Add some chili for heat, if preferred.

CHILLED CURRIED CHICKPEA SOUP

Serves 1 generously, or 2 modestly

This soup takes all of the warmth from a chickpea curry and makes it palatable for those days when the pavement burns the bottom of your feet. It pairs perfectly with a frosty ale and a sporting match you're only half interested in seeing the outcome of. Don't be tempted to scrimp on the turmeric chickpeas—they provide a delightful contrast of textures (though if you were pushed for time you could always lob on top a few of the Spiced Chickpea Bombs from page 44).

1 x 14-ounce can of chickpeas, rinsed
7 ounces cherry tomatoes
¾ tablespoon curry powder
1 lime
4 tablespoons Greek yogurt
4 ice cubes
2 tablespoons sunflower oil
1 teaspoon ground turmeric
small green or red chili, diced

Equipment
a blender that can crush ice cubes

Blend three-quarters of the chickpeas, all the cherry tomatoes and curry powder, the juice and zest of ½ the lime, 2 tablespoons of the Greek yogurt, and the ice cubes until smooth. If it is too chunky, add a couple of tablespoons of cold water. Chill the soup in the refrigerator until serving.

Heat the oil and turmeric in a skillet. Fry the remaining chickpeas until golden and crisp.

If you prefer a smoother, more elegant soup, now strain it through a strainer. Portion the soup into bowls. Top with a swirl of the remaining yogurt, a wedge of lime, the chili, and the turmeric chickpeas.

QUINOA AGUADITO, OR PERUVIAN CHICKEN, AND CILANTRO SOUP

Serves 2 to 3

This is not a soup for that portion of the population who thinks cilantro tastes unspeakably like soap. But for the rest of us, it can be something of a revelation. The first time a Peruvian friend made me aguadito, I was floored by the quantity of green fronds that found their way into the pot. It was bold and brash and something to behold, particularly the way the strong taste of cilantro was anchored by the silkiness of chicken stock and zip of lime and chili. And while the flavors may appear all light and bright, this is a soup that's deceptively filling, particularly if you take the liberties that I have by inserting green peas and quinoa. Quinoa isn't traditional in an aguadito, but to me it's a natural inclusion—combining two of Peru's most famed tastes together in a single bowl.

large bunch of fresh cilantro, well washed
1 onion
2 garlic cloves, peeled
3 tablespoons olive oil
4 cups chicken stock
½ cup quinoa, rinsed well
generous 1 cup frozen peas
2 raw chicken breasts or 12 ounces cooked chicken, shredded
1 teaspoon sea salt

To serve
2–3 lime wedges and finely chopped green chili (optional)

To prepare the cilantro, trim the very ends off the stems. Now roughly chop the stems and set the leaves aside for later.

Put the cilantro stems, onion, garlic, and 2 tablespoons of the olive oil in a food processor and blitz to a paste.

Place a saucepan over medium heat. Add the cilantro paste and fry for about 3 minutes to soften the onion and garlic.

Add the chicken stock to the pan and bring it to a boil. Add the quinoa, cover the pan with the lid, and simmer for 15 minutes. If you are using raw chicken, place it in the pot now to poach. After 15 minutes, or when the quinoa and chicken are cooked through, remove the chicken from the pan and shred it with 2 forks.

Add the frozen peas and shredded chicken to the pan and heat until the peas and chicken are piping hot.

Pound the reserved cilantro leaves, the remaining olive oil, and the salt together to a paste either using a mortar and pestle or a food processor. Stir this through the soup before serving it with lime wedges and if you fancy things to be a little hotter, green chili, to taste.

AJO BLANCO
WITH RED GRAPES

Serves 4

This is another soup traditionally bolstered with bread (this time from the south of Spain) which finds a new life with the inclusion of beans. The silky emulsion of blanched almonds, poached garlic, and infused milk is traditionally served cold with slivered grapes for sweetness. Green are classic, but the contrast of the red is what floats my boat. It also makes an elegant amuse-bouche in shot glasses, perhaps with pearls of pomegranate festooned on top; and by omitting the water it will also make a terrific warm sauce for roast fish, lamb, or chicken (try it with the sea bass on page 90). In order to get the right velvety smooth texture you will need a powerful blender, or if it's still a bit chunky, strain it before serving.

3 garlic cloves, peeled
generous 1 cup milk
generous ¾ cup blanched almonds
½ x 14-ounce can of cannellini beans, rinsed
1 teaspoon sea salt
½ cup water
2 tablespoons olive oil
1 teaspoon red wine vinegar
12 red grapes, cut into slivers

Put the garlic and milk in a saucepan over low–medium heat and bring to a simmer. Poach the garlic for about 7 minutes, or until the point of a knife can slide easily through it.

Put the infused milk, poached garlic, almonds, beans, and salt into a powerful blender or food processor. Blend until you have a paste. Drizzle in the water and continue to blend until you have a smooth, creamy consistency.

Drizzle in the olive oil and vinegar and blend to emulsify.

Serve the soup either lukewarm or chilled, with red grape slivers floating on the top of each portion.

GREEN SOUP WITH CHORIZO ALMOND CRUMBS

Serves 2 to 3

The nights when you crave something green often emerge from the pale plateau of jet lag. This soup's origins follow a late flight from Sydney. When I asked The Hungry One what he fancied for dinner, the answer was: "I should probably eat something green. But I'm a little too tired to chew." So that's how this Kermit-hued pot of joy was born. Here are a few guiding principles to help steer the course: treat the vegetables the same as if you were making a stir-fry (chop them roughly the same size so the cooking is quick and consistent); start sautéing the hardier ingredients before the delicate ones and don't overcook them; douse everything briefly in piping hot stock and remove it from the stove before it turns as brown and grim as a bunch of forgotten flowers.

You may question the inclusion of apple, but it does help to temper the bitterness of the brassicas. As for the chorizo and almonds—they're there just for a little spice and contrast but if you're keen on a vegetarian route, you can top it with some goat curd, lemon zest, and toasted pine nuts and you'll find it's just as restorative (if not even more so).

1 tablespoon olive oil
1 sweet red apple, peeled, cored, and diced
7 ounces (6 stems) tenderstem broccoli/broccolini, diced—including stems (you could also substitute with ½ head of broccoli)
1 zucchini, diced
scant 2 cups frozen peas
3 handfuls of kale, finely chopped
generous 2 cups hot vegetable or chicken stock
sea salt
2 tablespoons fresh flat-leaf parsley leaves

Chorizo crumble (optional)
1¾ ounces chorizo, crumbled by hand into small pieces
1–2 tablespoons olive oil and 1 teaspoon smoked paprika, if needed
2 tablespoons slivered almonds

Heat the olive oil in a heavy-bottom saucepan or Dutch oven over medium heat. Add the apple and sauté for 2 minutes. Add the broccoli and sauté for 2 to 4 minutes until it begins to soften.

Add the zucchini, peas, and kale and sauté for about 4 minutes, stirring so the peas defrost and the kale wilts.

Pour the hot stock into the pan and bring it to a simmer. Cover the pan with the lid and simmer until the apple and broccoli are soft.

Using a stick blender, food processor, or blender, blitz the contents of the pan until smooth. If you are using a food processor or blender, be careful—don't fill it all the way to the top and be sure to place a dish towel over the top of the blender while you blitz, as hot liquids can expand and spill out.

Taste and season with salt if needed.

To make the optional chorizo crumble, fry the chorizo in a skillet over medium heat until it is cooked through and has leached crimson oil into the pan. If there is none, then add the olive oil and smoked paprika. Add the slivered almonds and cook until the almonds have been toasted in the oil.

Serve the soup with the chorizo crumble and parsley scattered over the top.

If not a baked potato, then what? If not fluffy naan, boiled rice, hot fries, velvety mash, or an artful twirl of noodles, then what will occupy the lion's share of your dinner plate? The following are a collection of sides and salads that now take pride of place on our table. I'll often match one with a variety of simply broiled and roasted proteins, from slow-roasted lamb, to quickly broiled chicken skewers, a seared piece of steak or salmon, a square of steamed tofu, or a five-minute egg. They're worldly and fun, swift—and best yet—filling, made from either smart carbs, vegetables, or some sneaky protein. All of which means I've finally reached a stage where I can put a piece of broiled fish and one of the following on the table for dinner and The Hungry One will no longer look around and wonder what's for the main course.

INTERESTING SIDES & SALADS (FILLING ENOUGH TO FEED A 6'3" MAN)

SIMPLE PURÉES AS A BASE FOR PROTEIN (BYE BYE MASHED POTATO!)

It's the pliant squish of white carbs I found hardest to live without. What is a lamb cutlet without a bed of mashed potatoes, an osso bucco without a base of risotto Milanese, or a tagine without a downy tumble of couscous on the side?

One easy solution can be found in purées of other, lower-GI vegetables and beans. Simply steamed, wilted, or warmed through then blitzed with a stick blender, these six purées swiftly become simple building blocks for sturdy meals. Once you've got the basics mastered, all that's needed are some extra spices or herbs to twist them in an entirely new direction (try cumin or turmeric with the carrot, or mint or tarragon with the peas). And if your inspiration and inclination to cook start and end with a purée, never fear—slosh in an extra cup of water or stock and you've got yourself a bowl of soup. Dinner: sorted.

FENNEL PURÉE

Serves 2

1 teaspoon fennel seeds
4 tablespoons olive oil
1 medium fennel bulb (or 2 small ones),
   root and tips trimmed, diced
a pinch of sea salt

Add the fennel seeds to a dry skillet over medium heat and cook for 1 to 2 minutes, shaking frequently. Add half of the olive oil, the fennel, and salt and sauté for 7 to 10 minutes until the fennel has softened. Purée with the remaining olive oil until smooth.

<u>TO SERVE:</u> *Great as a base for fish or pork. With pork, try adding a peeled, cored, and diced Granny Smith apple to the pan.*

CAULIFLOWER PURÉE

Serves 6 (and freezes well)

1 head of cauliflower, green bits discarded,
   cut into small florets, and stem diced
generous 1 cup water
a pinch of sea salt
2 tablespoons olive oil

Put the cauliflower and water in a saucepan and bring to a simmer. Cover the pan with the lid and cook at a gentle simmer over medium heat for 15 minutes, stirring occasionally to prevent it catching or scorching. After 15 minutes, remove the lid and simmer for another 10 minutes, stirring occasionally until the cauliflower is soft. Purée with the salt and olive oil until smooth.

<u>TO SERVE:</u> *Shines when paired with steak, sausages, chicken, scallops, or roast lamb, or try it on its own with some herb oil or pesto drizzled over the top for a warming soup.*

PEA PURÉE

Serves 2

2¼ cups frozen peas
1½ tablespoons water
1 tablespoon olive oil
½ teaspoon sea salt

Put the peas and water in a saucepan over medium heat until the peas are hot through. Purée with the olive oil and salt and serve warm.

TO SERVE: *Lovely with pink fish, chicken, or lamb. Try adding a handful of fresh mint and a tablespoon of crumbled feta or a tablespoon of pesto. Alternatively, fry a tablespoon of green curry paste in the pan before adding the peas for a refreshing Asian alternative to rice alongside a whole baked fish.*

CARROT PURÉE

Serves 2

4 medium carrots, peeled and diced
1 tablespoon olive oil
½ teaspoon sea salt

Steam the carrots for 2 minutes or until they can be pierced with the tip of a knife. Purée with the olive oil and salt. Serve warm.

TO SERVE: *Terrific with roast beef, chicken, or white fish. Try adding 3 tablespoons hummus or 1 tablespoon tahini (sesame seed paste) for a Middle Eastern turn, or fresh, grated ginger for a bit of zip.*

WHITE BEAN PURÉE

Serves 4

2 x 14-ounce cans of cannellini beans, rinsed
1½ tablespoons milk
1 tablespoon olive oil
½ teaspoon salt

Blitz together the beans and milk using a stick blender or food processor, until smooth. Transfer the purée to a saucepan and gently heat, stirring often to prevent it from sticking to the pan. Season with salt and drizzle with olive oil just before serving.

TO SERVE: *Use whenever you would use mashed potato. Try adding roast garlic, or folding through kale and scallion for a take on colcannon (see page 142).*

SPLIT PEA PURÉE

Serves 4

1 cup dried yellow split peas, rinsed
1 fresh or dried bay leaf
3 garlic cloves, peeled
1 teaspoon sea salt
4 tablespoons extra virgin olive oil
2 tablespoons good-quality red wine vinegar

Put the split peas in a large saucepan over high heat and add enough cold water to cover the peas by 2 inches. Bring to a boil, then reduce the heat to medium and cook for 5 minutes. Skim off any scum that forms on the surface using a spoon. Add the bay leaf and garlic cloves and simmer for 40 minutes. Add the salt and simmer for 20 more minutes until the peas are soft. Drain any excess liquid and remove the bay leaf. Purée with the olive oil and vinegar until very smooth.

TO SERVE: *This Greek-inspired purée is lovely with flash-fried capers over the top and as a side to broiled lamb skewers or simple broiled fish or squid. It's also lovely as a dip with crudités and a bowl of olives.*

BROCCOLI STEAKS WITH CHIMICHURRI AND BRAZIL NUTS

Serves 4

Being in the great parrillas of Buenos Aires and not being able to face meat can be a cruel curse. Yet that's what can happen when your adventures in South America coincide with the full throes of morning/all-day sickness. There were many nights when I was caught between a rock of bleeding-rare steaks and the hard place of stodgy pastas when I wished this broccoli dish was on offer. By cleaving a head of broccoli into "steaks" and charring it on a grill you not only have some visual novelty (it closely resembles the transverse of a tree), but it brings out the brassica's inherent meaty and nutty taste. The accompanying chimichurri is a trilling South American sauce traditionally served with steaks; it's a busy slurry of herbs, heat, and here, the vibrancy of orange. Serve it over the broccoli, but also don't be shy about sloshing it over a piece of red meat or two. These days I like a sirloin steak, medium-rare.

1–2 heads of broccoli/1¼ pounds, stems trimmed 1¼ inches below the florets and remaining head of broccoli cleaved vertically into 4 "steaks" approximately ¾ inch thick
2 tablespoons olive oil
1 teaspoon crushed red pepper flakes
¼ cup Brazil nuts, roughly chopped
sea salt

Chimichurri
handful of picked fresh flat-leaf parsley leaves
handful of picked fresh oregano leaves
handful of picked fresh cilantro leaves
1 tablespoon finely chopped cilantro stems
½ garlic clove, peeled
¼ cup good-quality olive oil
grated zest of ½ orange
2 tablespoons orange juice
1 teaspoon red wine vinegar
fresh chili, to taste

To make the chimichurri, put the fresh herbs, garlic, and olive oil in a blender or food processor. Whizz until smooth. Add the orange zest and juice, and the vinegar. Briefly blend to combine.

Add salt and chili to taste (I wouldn't be shy about either of them). If you think it can handle more garlic, grate a little more in, but be careful—the flavor will become stronger over time.

To cook the broccoli, preheat a barbecue/grill pan to medium–high. Brush each "steak" with the olive oil, sprinkle with the red pepper flakes and season with salt. Barbecue with the hood down over the barbecue, or griddle with a metal bowl covering the steaks until lightly charred and cooked through—about 5 to 6 minutes per side. Serve the charred broccoli drizzled with chimichurri and sprinkled with the Brazil nuts, for crunch.

SAVORY BAKED APPLES WITH GOAT CURD AND PROSCIUTTO

Serves 6

Baked apples, stuffed with butter, cinnamon, walnuts, currants, and almonds were a favorite dessert of my late English grandmother. She served them warm with cold custard, the outsides of the apples as wrinkled as the backs of her hands. Here I've taken them on a savory route. They provide a lovely companion for a bitter green salad, perhaps with roast chicken as a centerpiece. You can use most red apples, which have a good crunch and bite. Green may prove a little too tart. You could also substitute the goat curd mix for skinned sausage meat for a heartier twist, or swap the goat curd for blue cheese if you want something richer. The lavender, while not essential at all, does add a subtle floral note to the goat curd, which in turn picks up some of the country-lane-sweetness in a Royal Gala apple.

6 small red eating apples (I like Royal Gala)
8 slices (3¼ ounces) of prosciutto, 6 cut in half lengthwise,
   2 cut into thirds to create large postage-stamp squares
scant ¼ cup hazelnuts, toasted and roughly chopped
scant ¼ cup almonds, toasted and roughly chopped
¾ cup goat curd
1 tablespoon finely chopped fresh rosemary leaves
a pinch of unsprayed lavender leaves (optional)
a drizzle of olive oil
scant 1 cup apple cider or apple juice
sea salt and freshly ground black pepper
a handful of salad greens per person

Equipment
apple corer or melon baller

Preheat the oven to 300°F.

Cut the tops off the apples, about ½ inch below the stalk, then set the tops aside. Use an apple corer or a melon baller to remove the core of the apple and fashion a tunnel about as thick as a wine cork through the center. You want the walls of the remaining apple to be ⅝ inch thick. Discard the cores. Using a sharp knife, score a shallow slit around the perimeter of each apple, about ½ inch below the top (this will prevent the apples from bursting during baking).

Take one postage-stamp square of ham and shimmy it down to the bottom of the tunnel and let the corners snake up the sides—you want to create a "plug" for the filling so it doesn't fall out the bottom during baking.

Combine the chopped nuts with the goat curd, rosemary, and lavender, if you fancy. Add the olive oil and mash with a fork to combine. Season with salt and pepper.

Divide the filling into 6 portions and press each portion into the hollow in each apple, being careful not to push out the ham plug at the bottom.

Wrap 2 sheets of prosciutto around each apple. Use the fattiest parts of ham as glue to help it stick to the fruit. If it really won't stick, you can always use a toothpick to fasten it in place.

Put the apples in a baking dish and drizzle the tops with a little olive oil. Pour the cider or apple juice into the baking dish and place the tops of the apples in there too.

Cover the dish with foil (try not to let the foil touch the filling) and bake in the preheated oven for 40 minutes. Remove the foil, turn the oven temperature up to 350°F and bake for another 20 minutes or until the apples are soft and the ham is crisp.

Serve the apples warm, with the tops at a jaunty angle for presentation, with salad greens and a drizzling of the cooking juices from the bottom of the dish.

BRUSSELS SPROUTS WITH HAZELNUTS, LENTILS, AND MUSTARD DRESSING

Serves 4

I finally got my taste of Buenos Aires in Sydney of all places. Porteño in Surry Hills is the parrilla you dreamed of finding in San Telmo, but never quite happened upon. Besides the whole beasts that loll over a wood-burning fire, what they're famed for are their Brussels sprouts, which are deep fried, and magical. This is a slightly lighter version using the heat of the oven, with some chew and sweetness coming from pairing them with dried apple and hazelnuts.
I like to eat them with some broiled lamb or beef, but for a vegetarian twist, try them with the Broccoli Steaks with Chimichurri and Brazil Nuts on page 68. Tango tunes in the background are entirely optional.

1 pound 2 ounces Brussels sprouts, bases trimmed, and cut in half
4 tablespoons olive oil
a generous pinch of sea salt
scant ½ cup hazelnuts, roughly chopped (in half is fine)
2 tablespoons finely chopped dried apple (optional)
handful of fresh flat-leaf parsley, roughly chopped

Dressed lentils
¼ cup small French green lentils, e.g. Puy lentils
scant ¼ cup extra virgin olive oil
2 tablespoons apple cider vinegar
2 tablespoons brown sugar
1–2 teaspoons hot English mustard (or Dijon if you prefer a milder flavor)

Preheat the oven to 400°F.

Place the Brussels sprouts, cut side up, snugly in a baking dish. Drizzle with the olive oil and season with the salt. Scatter the hazelnuts around the sprouts. Bake them in the preheated oven for 40 minutes, or until the tops are bronzed and the centers are soft.

While the sprouts are roasting, make the dressed lentils. Rinse the lentils well and place them in a saucepan with enough cold water to cover them by ¾ inch. Bring the water to a boil and cook the lentils for 15 to 20 minutes, until just tender.

Whisk together the oil, vinegar, brown sugar, and mustard in a small saucepan over low heat until it barely simmers. You want it to be both emulsified and warmed through. Taste it. If you like a stronger mustard flavor, add another teaspoon and whisk it well to combine.

Drain the cooked lentils, add them to the warm dressing, and toss to combine. If you fancy the dried apple, add it now as well.

Scatter the dressed lentils over the top of the roasted sprouts and hazelnuts. Top with the parsley.

TIP: *If you were pressed for time you could easily substitute the Puy lentils for a can of lentils, rinsed, well drained, and then combined with the warm dressing in a saucepan to gently heat them through.*

CAULIFLOWER AND BROCCOLI GRATIN

Serves 4

A cauliflower or broccoli "cheese" was my definition of childhood comfort—probably because one of the first things my mother taught me to make was béchamel. I remember sitting on the kitchen bench and watching her methodically stirring the warmed milk into the roux, coaxing it into a silky consistency. It would then be poured over broccoli and cauliflower florets and baked until the top puckered and blistered. This dish goes a slightly different route and has a sneaky substitution of a cheese-gilded cauliflower purée as the sauce. Look, mom! No flour! You'd be hard pressed to taste the difference. Instead, it's a concentrated combination of soft and crisp vegetables, a little dairy and still plenty of satisfying squish. It's comfort food at its best (and is lovely with chicken, steak, or good-quality sausages).

14 ounces cauliflower, green bits discarded, cut into small
   florets, and stem diced
scant 1 cup water
1 cup grated mozzarella or provolone cheese
1 large head of broccoli (1 pound 7 ounces), cut into florets
scant ⅓ cup grated Parmesan
¼ cup slivered almonds
a pinch of crushed red pepper flakes (optional)
sea salt

Put the cauliflower and water in a saucepan, cover with the lid, and simmer over medium heat for 15 minutes, stirring occasionally to prevent it catching or scorching. Remove the lid and simmer for another 10 minutes, or until the cauliflower is soft, stirring occasionally. Season with a pinch of salt, then use a stick blender or food processor to blend the cauliflower to a smooth cream.

Return the cauliflower purée to the saucepan and add the mozzarella or provolone. Stir over low heat until the cheese has melted through.

Preheat a broiler to high.

Steam the broccoli for 3 minutes or until al dente.

Transfer the broccoli to a baking dish and pour the cheesy cauliflower sauce over it. Sprinkle the top with the Parmesan and slivered almonds. Place under the broiler for 7 minutes or until the top has bronzed and the almonds have browned. Add red pepper flakes if you want an extra kick, and serve hot.

CHICKPEAS, LEEK, APPLE, AND PEAR SALAD

Serves 2

This is a warming fall tangle, with the sweetness of the leeks amplified by slivers of dried pear and crisp apple. The simple process of introducing the fennel seeds and garlic to the olive oil over medium heat helps them to infuse and creates a lovely base for a dressing. While the chickpeas add some structure, you could easily substitute them for white beans or steamed segments of cauliflower. I often find myself serving this as a side dish to the Blue Cheese Soufflés (page 120) on a Sunday night when the air is starting to nip, following it up with a portion of the Rhubarb, Apple, and Berry Slow Crumble (page 167).

1 tablespoon fennel seeds
4 tablespoons olive oil
2 garlic cloves, peeled and thinly sliced
1 leek, cut in half lengthwise, rinsed and sliced
  1¼ inches thick
1 x 14-ounce can of chickpeas, rinsed
3 tablespoons dried pear, finely sliced
1 tablespoon apple cider vinegar
2 tablespoons almonds, toasted and roughly chopped
½ Pink Lady apple, cut into very thin slivers
sea salt and freshly ground black pepper

Place a skillet over medium heat, add the fennel seeds, and toast for 1 minute.

Add half the olive oil and the garlic. Turn down the heat and sauté for 2 minutes, being careful not to scorch the garlic. Add the leek and cook for 8 to 10 minutes until soft, then add the chickpeas to warm through.

Toss the contents of the pan with the dried pear. Season with salt and pepper and dress with the remaining olive oil and the vinegar. Top with the toasted almonds and slivers of apple.

"THREE BEANS" WITH BASIL PESTO

Serves 4

Green beans with pesto is a classic combination in Liguria, where it's often paired with a double white-starch hit of pasta and potato. If you're after something a little lighter, try this version of a three-bean salad. There's still the textural crunch of the green beans against a slick basil sauce, but the inclusion of borlotti and white beans make for a more sustaining energy boost (you could also substitute the borlotti beans for black beans). Serve this either warm or cold, as part of an antipasto platter with roasted tomatoes, olives, and eggplant, or as a simple side dish to broiled chicken or roast lamb.

generous 3¾ cups fresh basil leaves
⅓ cup pine nuts, toasted
½ cup extra virgin olive oil
generous ⅓ cup finely grated Parmesan
2 garlic cloves, peeled and grated
juice of ½ lemon
1 x 14-ounce can of borlotti or black beans, rinsed
1 x 14-ounce can of cannellini or other white beans, rinsed
11 ounces green beans, trimmed and cut into thirds
2 tablespoons pumpkin seeds
sea salt and freshly ground black pepper

Make a pesto by pounding the basil, pine nuts, olive oil, Parmesan, garlic, and lemon juice together either with a mortar and pestle or blitzing them to a paste in a food processor. Check the seasoning and adjust to taste.

Place all 3 sets of beans in a saucepan and warm them with the pesto over low heat until the green beans are cooked but still retain some bite. Don't cook for too long, as the pesto may turn an unsightly shade of brown.

Serve the salad warm with the pumpkin seeds scattered over the top.

CAULIFLOWER "COUSCOUS" WITH ALMONDS, CURRANTS, AND MINT

Serves 4 to 6

This is a nifty trick. It turns out that by grating a cauliflower or giving it a swift tumble in a food processor, you can transform its rubbly nodules into small grains that closely resemble couscous. You can serve it raw, but I find a few minutes in a skillet help to coax the best flavor out of them. From there, the rest is pure instinct. This salad takes its cue from my favorite way to consume couscous. The currants are plumped up by the bergamot tannins in Earl Grey tea and the almonds and herbs provide the necessary color and texture. You can try serving this under a tagine (perhaps the Lamb Shank and Fig Tagine on page 128) or on its own with a tahini-yogurt dressing and some barbecued chicken, fish or lamb. Incidentally, the tahini-yogurt dressing also makes an excellent marinade for chicken or lamb. Try making double and leaving the proteins to marinate in the refrigerator for 30 minutes before baking or broiling them.

½ cup currants
½ cup strong, hot Earl Grey tea
2 tablespoons olive oil
1 large head of cauliflower, grated on a box grater into small
    fragments like chubby couscous grains (1 head should
    provide approximately 4 cups)
a pinch of sea salt
grated zest and juice of ½ lemon
scant ½ cup slivered almonds, toasted and chopped
small bunch of fresh flat-leaf parsley, chopped
small bunch of fresh mint, chopped

Tahini-yogurt dressing
1 tablespoon tahini (sesame seed paste)
⅔ cup Greek yogurt
1 tablespoon olive oil
grated zest and juice of ½ lemon

Soak the currants in the Earl Grey tea for 10 to 15 minutes until they have plumped up.

In the meantime, place a large skillet over medium heat and add the olive oil, cauliflower grains, and salt. Sauté for 5 minutes to help remove the raw taste from the cauliflower.

Transfer the contents of the pan to a bowl with the lemon zest and juice, almonds, fresh herbs, and plumped, drained currants. Stir to combine.

To make the tahini-yogurt dressing, mix all the ingredients together to combine.

Serve the "couscous" with the tahini-yogurt dressing on the side, or underneath a tagine.

DAL

Serves 2 as a main or 4 as a side

A great dal recipe is an asset for life. A note: while yellow split peas and chana dal look very similar, they are different (if you look closely, dal have a rippled exterior). It's the yellow split peas which cook down to mush more quickly, whereas the hardier dal will allow you to take a hand whisk to them after cooking, providing a good textural mix of rough and smooth. In order to insert a good jolt of flavor, cook the tarka seasoning separately and then fold it through at the end. The apple cider vinegar is not a traditional inclusion, but I think you'll find it does wonders.

generous 1 cup chana dal, soaked in generous 2 cups water
  for 1 hour
3½ cups water
1 teaspoon ground turmeric

Tarka seasoning
1 onion, peeled
3 Roma tomatoes
2 garlic cloves, peeled
2 tablespoons neutral-tasting oil
1 tablespoon ground cumin
1 teaspoon ground turmeric
1 teaspoon ground coriander
½ teaspoon ground cinnamon
1 teaspoon ground ginger
1 teaspoon sea salt
1 tablespoon apple cider vinegar

To serve
fresh cilantro and chopped red chili

Drain the soaked dal and rinse it well until the water runs clear.

Put the dal in a heavy-bottom saucepan or Dutch oven with the water and turmeric. Set over medium heat and bring to a boil, skimming off any froth that forms on the surface using a spoon. Lower the heat so that the water is just simmering and clamp on a lid. Cook for about 40 minutes, checking occasionally to make sure there is still enough liquid in the pan. When the dal is pliable and there's a scant amount of liquid left, take the pan off the heat. (If the dal is soft but you still have an excess of water, drain off all but about scant ½ cup of the cooking liquid.) Use a whisk to form a rough purée out of the dal and liquid.

To make the tarka seasoning, use a food processor to blitz the onion, tomatoes, and garlic to a paste.

Heat the oil in a skillet and fry all the spices for 1 to 2 minutes, until fragrant. Add the onion-tomato paste and cook over medium heat for 2 to 3 minutes until everything has darkened and the raw onion taste has disappeared.

Stir the tarka seasoning, salt, and vinegar into the dal and heat through before serving with cilantro and chili sprinkled over the top.

SMOKY EGGPLANT WITH TOMATOES, PICKLED ONION, PARSLEY, AND POMEGRANATE MOLASSES

Serves 4

This dish transports me straight to Zübeyir Ocakbaşi, a historic terrace in Istanbul, on a side street near the main shopping boulevard of Istiklal Caddesi. You can smell the restaurant before you see it, as most of the food is grilled over coals in the center of the downstairs dining room. This side is a slightly more refined version of their "Special Eggplant Salad." Here it's accented with the crunch of walnuts and sweetness of softened onions. Over time I've discovered the best way to get the soft texture and smoky aroma in the eggplant is to place it whole, directly over a gas burner, occasionally turning it until the skin is withered and the insides are as pulpy as an overripe piece of fruit. I like to eat this with simple charred meat or offal (in Istanbul we had skewers of liver, which were sublime) and perhaps the Cauliflower "Couscous" with Almonds, Currants, and Mint (page 76) as part of a wider mezze or barbecue feast for a group.

1 red onion, peeled and cut into half-moons,
   as slim as you can manage
1 teaspoon sea salt
2 tablespoons red wine vinegar
2 large eggplants
2 tablespoons olive oil
2-inch lump of ginger root, peeled and grated
1 brown onion, peeled and cut into slim half-moons
2 tablespoons pomegranate molasses
2 tablespoons water
2 Roma tomatoes, diced
small handful of fresh flat-leaf parsley, chopped
½ cup walnuts, roughly chopped
sea salt and freshly ground black pepper

To serve
labneh, feta, soft eggs, or broiled lamb (optional)

Place half of the red onion in a bowl with the salt and vinegar. Let the onion steep for 15 to 30 minutes until it has begun to turn translucent and the raw taste has softened.

Using tongs or similar, carefully hold an eggplant directly over a gas burner. Let it char for 5 minutes on each side, until the skin is black and puckered and the insides feel pulpy and soft. Transfer it to a bowl and cover the bowl with plastic wrap. Repeat this with the other eggplant and add it to the bowl, too.

Leave the charred eggplants to sit and steam under the plastic wrap for 10 to 15 minutes while you get started on the rest of the sauce.

Heat the olive oil in a skillet or wok and add the ginger, brown onion, and the remaining, raw red onion. Sauté over medium heat for 10 minutes, or until the onions have softened. Add the pomegranate molasses and water and sauté for another 5 to 10 minutes until you have a soft, pliable tangle of onions.

Remove the eggplants from the bowl, peel off the charred skins, and discard them. Roughly chop the softened, smoked flesh and combine it with the onions in the pan to warm it through. Taste and season with salt and pepper if needed.

Top the warm mixture with the tomatoes, pickled and drained red onion, parsley, and walnuts. Serve either warm or at room temperature, with labneh, feta, soft eggs, or broiled lamb, if you like.

ROAST BEET AND CARROTS WITH RAS EL HANOUT, MINT, AND LABNEH

Serves 2 (or 4 if paired with the recipe to the right, here)

Beet and carrots may skirt a little higher in the GI stakes than some vegetables, but this sweet and jeweled combination of them with the freshness of mint and labneh, is just too good to miss—particularly when coupled with a ras el hanout spice blend (which translates as "top of the shop" and may include up to 30 aromatics). The smell of it all transports me straight back to the souks of Marrakech. I like to treat this dish as an adornment to a meal, perhaps serving it with a sustaining base of the yellow split peas (to the right) and some chicken or lamb kebabs from the barbecue.

4 medium carrots (about 1 pound), peeled
1 tablespoon orange marmalade
4 tablespoons olive oil
8 small cooked baby beets (5½ ounces), drained (from a can or package will suffice)
2 teaspoons sea salt flakes
2 tablespoons ras el hanout
scant ¼ cup slivered almonds, toasted
2 tablespoons labneh (strained Greek yogurt) or goat feta, crumbled
20 fresh mint leaves, torn

Preheat the oven to 400°F.

Cut 3½ of the carrots into thin sticks. Set the remaining half-carrot aside.

In a small saucepan, combine the marmalade and olive oil. Warm it gently and whisk it to emulsify.

Combine the carrot sticks and beet in a roasting dish with the marmalade mixture and sprinkle with the salt and ras el hanout. Roast in the preheated oven for 50 minutes or until the vegetables have taken on a burnished hue and are cooked through.

Shave the remaining half-carrot into ribbons using a vegetable peeler.

Serve the roasted vegetables with the almonds, labneh, carrot ribbons, and mint leaves scattered over the top.

YELLOW SPLIT PEAS WITH BURNED BUTTER AND ORANGE

Serves 4

This dish is the taste of sunshine. There's warmth from the ginger and chili and some exuberance from the orange. By simply drizzling the beans with a nut-brown butter that's primped with garlic and toasted almonds, somehow it elevates a slick of yellow peas into something stunning. When I'm not serving this dish alongside the Roast Beet and Carrots with Ras el Hanout, Mint, and Labneh (opposite) and some protein, fresh from the barbecue, I like to eat it as is, topped with a five-minute egg so the orange yolk can slowly seep into the base, blurring orange into yellow, creating a molten tumble of warmth.

1 tablespoon olive oil
1 red onion, peeled, halved, and cut into thin slivers
2-inch lump of ginger root, peeled
2 red chili peppers, 1 halved, 1 finely diced
½ orange
1 cup yellow split peas, rinsed
1¾ cups hot water

Burned butter
1 teaspoon olive oil
2 garlic cloves, peeled and thinly sliced
2 tablespoons butter
2 tablespoons almonds, roughly chopped into thirds

To serve
2 tablespoons plain yogurt, and chia seeds (optional)

Heat the olive oil in a heavy-bottom saucepan or Dutch oven over medium heat. Add the onion, ginger, the halved chili, and the orange, cut side down, and sauté for 7 to 10 minutes until the onion has softened and the orange is starting to gain some color. Add the split peas and hot water and bring to a boil. Cover the pan with the lid and simmer for 45 minutes, or until the liquid has largely been absorbed and the split peas have cooked but not completely broken down. (If there is an excess of liquid and the peas have cooked, drain some of the liquid.) Squeeze any remaining juice from the orange into the pan, then remove it and the lump of ginger.

For the burned butter, put the olive oil, garlic, diced chili, butter, and almonds into a skillet over medium heat. Heat until the butter has turned nut-brown.

Serve the split peas with a drizzle of yogurt and the burned butter. Sprinkle over some chia seeds if preferred.

BLACK BEAN, CHORIZO, SWEET POTATO, AND COCONUT BOWL

Serves 2

Out of all of the beans that play hide and seek in cans at the back of your pantry, black beans may be my favorite. To liven up this chunky salad I add red onion in two textures—softly roasted and thinly sliced and raw. There's a tiny touch of chorizo for richness (though if you wanted to skip the pork and fat, smoked paprika sprinkled over the sweet potato would also work nicely). And then there are some green herbs and yogurt to link it all together. It's lovely piping hot and just as good at room temperature. Here are some more good things about it: you can happily eat it out of a bowl with a fork; you could easily add some chicken, shrimp, or squid for extra protein; and at the very end you'll only find one pan to wash up. Like all warm salads like this, the quantities and combinations of flavors are a little fluid. If you don't have sweet potato, but have pumpkin, substitute it. If you hate cilantro, then swap it for mint. If you can't find coconut shavings then slivered almonds would also work well.

1 large sweet potato, peeled and cubed
2 tablespoons olive oil
1¾ ounces chorizo, cut into thin coins and then in half (if vegetarian, omit this and sprinkle the sweet potato with 1 teaspoon ground cumin and 1 teaspoon smoked paprika)
handful of dried coconut shavings
1 red onion, peeled and cut into eighths
1 x 14-ounce can of black beans, rinsed
handful of fresh cilantro (or mint if you hate cilantro)
1 red chili, thinly sliced
Greek yogurt, to drizzle (optional)
sea salt and freshly ground black pepper

Preheat the oven to 350°F.

Place the sweet potato in a roasting tray, drizzle with the olive oil, and season with salt. Roast it in the preheated oven for 20 minutes or until it's gained a little color around the edges.

After 20 minutes, add the chorizo, coconut shavings, and most of the onion (leave one-eighth aside to sliver raw at the end). Roast for 20 minutes.

When the potato is cooked through and the onion has been stained slightly pink from the chorizo's oil, remove the tray from the oven and mix in the black beans. The heat from the roasting tray and its contents will help warm the beans.

Cut the remaining onion pieces into slivers as thin you can manage. Add the onion slivers, cilantro, and chili to the roasting tray.

Season with salt and pepper and drizzle Greek yogurt over the top before serving.

KALE CAESAR

Serves 4 to 6

There's more to this salad than the punning novelty of its name (though it is also something to hail). It takes that 90s cafe favorite and updates it with crispy chickpeas standing in for croutons, and raw, fine ribbons of kale for romaine. If you're searching for a little more substance, add in some soft egg or broiled chicken (since we've tinkered with everything else, this is hardly the time to get snippy about whether chicken has any place in a true Caesar salad). If you're not up to eating raw egg yolks (pregnant, immune compromised, etc.), then you can always whizz the capers, anchovies, and lemon zest through store-bought whole-egg mayonnaise and thin it with lemon juice until you get the right consistency.

3 slices of bacon, cut into thin sticks
1 x 14-ounce can of chickpeas, rinsed
1 tablespoon olive oil
14 ounces kale, hard stems discarded and leaves shredded into ribbons ¼ inch wide
1½ ounces Parmesan, shaved

Dressing
1 egg yolk
2 teaspoons Dijon mustard
1 garlic clove, peeled
2 teaspoons capers, drained
2 marinated anchovy fillets in oil, drained
¾ cup sunflower oil
grated zest and juice of 1 lemon
sea salt and freshly ground black pepper

To serve
2 hard-boiled eggs, or cooked or broiled chicken (optional)

Preheat the oven to 425°F.

Put the bacon and chickpeas on a baking sheet and drizzle with the olive oil. Bake in the preheated oven for 20 minutes, or until the bacon is very crisp and the chickpeas have developed a brittle crust.

To make the dressing, combine the egg yolk, mustard, garlic clove, capers, and anchovies in a blender and blend until smooth. Slowly drip in the oil, drop by drop, to make a dressing. Then drizzle in the lemon juice and whizz for a few seconds to combine. Season with salt and pepper.

Combine the kale with the lemon zest and the dressing. Top with the crispy bacon, chickpeas, and the Parmesan shavings.

If you fancy a little more protein, grate or break the hard-boiled eggs over the top of the salad, or mix through some shredded cooked chicken.

GADO GADO INDONESIAN VEGETABLE SALAD WITH SPICY PEANUT SAUCE

Serves 2

I should say upfront that this version of the classic Indonesian vegetable salad topped with satay sauce is much closer to what I made when I was studying Bahasa as a 13-year-old in Sydney than what you'd find in a kantin in Jakarta. But at its heart what remains is a great way to gussy up greens and the like when you just can't face one more stir-fry. You can substitute whichever vegetables you prefer: carrot sticks and zucchini would make fine additions. The traditional iteration will have a more exotic blend of roots and spices. It will also commonly play host to hard-boiled eggs. On a Wednesday night I prefer this quick version. I also like how the runny yolk in a five-minute egg adds a golden gloss to the dressing. Serve this on its own, or as a more substantial side for broiled chicken or fish.

3½ ounces snow peas, cut into thirds
3½ ounces broccoli or broccolini, cut into manageable pieces
1 red bell pepper, seeded and cut into thin sticks
¼ white cabbage, finely shredded
½ cup bean sprouts
2 eggs, boiled for 5 minutes, then plunged into cold water and shelled

Spicy peanut sauce
3 tablespoons peanut butter (crunchy or smooth)
2 tablespoons cashews
grated zest and juice of 1 lime
¾-inch lump of ginger root, peeled and grated
1 garlic clove, peeled and grated
1 small red chili, seeded and chopped
3 tablespoons water
1½ teaspoons light soy sauce
a pinch of sugar

Lightly steam the snow peas and broccoli or broccolini until they are soft but still retain some bite. Combine the steamed vegetables with the raw red bell pepper, cabbage, and bean sprouts and divide between 2 plates.

To make the spicy peanut sauce, put all the ingredients in a food processor and whizz to a paste.

Dab the plates of salad with the sauce. Place the peeled, boiled egg in the center of the plate and allow people to puncture their own yolk.

BORLOTTI BEANS WITH ROASTED PEAR, WALNUTS, AND BLUE CHEESE

Serves 2

To me, borlotti beans are the strong, silent member of the bean clan. Faintly brown and meekly nutty, they need to marry with some stronger flavors before they really begin to shine. This simple tray bake calls on the flavors you'd find on a good cheese board and throws them together. Red onion and burnished pear provide plump sweetness. There's the crumble of toasted almonds. And then there are small nuggets of blue cheese. I prefer Saint Agur, a not too assertive blue from the Auvergne region of France, though feel free to experiment with whichever type you prefer. This is a dish that pairs nicely with cooked chicken thighs as a warm salad, or if you're feeling jolly, double or triple it and serve it alongside a roast turkey.

2 tablespoons extra virgin olive oil
1 x 14-ounce can of borlotti beans, rinsed
1 red onion, peeled and cut into eighths
handful of walnuts
2 medium pears, cored and cut into eighths
2 handfuls of green leaves (e.g. arugula, baby spinach, watercress)
1½ ounces blue cheese
juice of ½ lemon

Preheat the oven to 325°F.

Drizzle half the olive oil into a baking dish and scatter the borlotti beans over it.

Top with the onion, walnuts, and three-quarters of the pear wedges. Drizzle with the remaining olive oil.

Bake in the preheated oven for about 1 hour, or until the onion pieces are soft, the walnuts toasted, and the pear softened.

Combine all the contents of the baking dish with the green leaves. Shave the remaining pieces of pear into ribbons using a vegetable peeler and scatter over the top. Crumble in the blue cheese and dress with a little lemon juice just before serving.

This is bright food, designed for long days and languid nights. It's the sort of supper you don't mind making when you know that there's a good chance tomorrow will involve either a bathing suit or a pair of shorts. In these pages are the sorts of feasts which take me on vacation even if I'm tethered to the kitchen. As soon as I'm sitting down to a plate of Thai green papaya salad, piri piri chicken, or Moroccan lamb and chickpea burgers, I'm elsewhere. And on the nights when The Hungry One and I are standing watch by the barbecue, supervising the production of griddled chili peppers stuffed with feta and black beans, or tandoori salmon with spiced lentils, we're never happier to be home.

LEAN SUMMER FEASTS

SEA BASS SWADDLED IN ZUCCHINI RIBBONS

Serves 2

Those with a garden will understand the plight: what do you do with the end-of-season glut of zucchini? Once, you might have snuck them into cakes or breads. Certainly, you can sauté slices by the stack, or practice your pickles. But might I suggest you put them to work here? Swaddling a skinless fillet of fish in overlapping strips of green and white calls for just a few minutes of craft with a vegetable peeler, but leaves a lasting visual impression. One other bonus is how it protects the delicate flesh of white fish fillets from the heat of a broiler or a pan. I find it's worth getting a good char on the crust to contrast with the pliant "noodle salad" on the side, which is made from the remaining ribbons of zucchini and glossed with a perky salsa verde. Additionally, ribbons of zucchini make an excellent substitution for noodles in many dishes—try them wafting in chicken or miso soup, or dressed with pesto for a lighter version of pasta.

2–3 medium zucchini
2 fillets of skinless sea bass or other white-fleshed fish, about 3½ ounces each
1 lemon, halved
1 tablespoon olive oil
handful of slivered almonds, toasted
sea salt

Parsley and tarragon salsa verde
small handful of fresh tarragon leaves
large handful of fresh flat-leaf parsley leaves
¼ cup olive oil
½ garlic clove, peeled and grated
2 marinated anchovy fillets in oil, drained
1 teaspoon capers, drained
juice of ½ lemon

Using a vegetable peeler or mandoline, shred the zucchini lengthwise into ribbons.

Pat the fish fillets dry with paper towels. Take a piece of parchment paper and lay out 12 overlapping ribbons of zucchini side by side on the paper. Place a fish fillet horizontally across the zucchini ribbons and use the paper to help swaddle the fillet in the ribbons. Turn the fish seam-side down. Repeat with 12 more ribbons and the second fish fillet. Place the fillets in the refrigerator until you are ready to cook them.

To make the parsley and tarragon salsa verde, whizz all the ingredients together in a food processor. Taste and season with salt and whizz again until you have a zippy slurry you are happy with.

Combine the remaining zucchini ribbons with the salsa verde and divide between 2 plates.

To cook the fish, place a large skillet over medium–high heat. You can test if the pan's surface is hot enough by placing the lemon halves, cut side down, in the pan. When it is ready, they should sizzle. Drizzle the olive oil in the hot pan, then add the fish fillets, seam-side down. Cook them for 3 to 5 minutes, until the ribbons have taken on some char. Gently flip them over, trying not to unravel the ribbons, and cook them for 2 minutes on the other side until the fish has cooked through.

Serve the pan-fried fish with the burnished lemon halves, dressed zucchini ribbons, and slivered almonds. If you need something else on the side, some steamed green beans, White Bean Purée (page 67), Fennel Purée (page 66), or Cauliflower Purée (page 66) would do nicely.

VITELLO TONNATO WITH GREEN BEAN AND TOMATO SALAD

Serves 6

This dish is protein, squared. It translates as slices of lean veal, seasoned with a sauce made from tuna. Before you turn the page in disbelief, bear with me. This is a classic Piedmontese combination, often served as part of an antipasto platter. Here it's repurposed as a main course that's perfect for a small group. Just sear the nut of veal, then leave it in the oven or on the barbecue to roast while you make the sauce and assemble the salad. What you get in the end is a canny combination; somehow the mellow meat finds new life with the briny acidity of the tuna sauce.

4-pound nut of veal (a boneless cut from the leg)
  at room temperature
2 teaspoons sea salt
1 teaspoon freshly ground black pepper
2 tablespoons olive oil

Tuna sauce
2 egg yolks
1 teaspoon Dijon mustard
⅔ cup neutral-tasting oil
1 tablespoon capers, drained
2 marinated anchovy fillets in oil, drained
6½ ounces canned tuna in olive oil
juice of ½ lemon

Salad
11 ounces green beans, steamed
4 tomatoes, sliced
1 red onion, peeled and cut into slivers
1 small bunch of fresh basil
2 tablespoons olive oil
1 teaspoon red wine vinegar

To serve
2 tablespoons capers, patted dry and fried in 2 tablespoons
  olive oil until they open up like flowers

Preheat a barbecue with a hood, or your oven to 325°F.

Season the veal with the salt and pepper. Drizzle the oil into either the flat plate of a barbecue or a skillet over medium heat and sear the meat for 2 minutes on each side to form a nice brown crust.

Transfer the meat to a baking dish and place it in the preheated oven or simply pull down the hood of the barbecue to roast. Cook it for 1 hour and 15 minutes, or until the internal temperature is 130–140°F. Let the meat rest somewhere warm and under foil for 20 to 30 minutes before carving. The meat will continue to cook through as it rests. The ends will be more done and the center pink.

To make the tuna sauce, put the egg yolks and mustard in a food processor and whizz to combine. With the motor running, slowly trickle in the oil, drop by drop, to create a mayonnaise. Once it has emulsified to a mayonnaise, add the capers, anchovies, tuna, and its marinating oil, and lemon juice, and blitz to combine.

To make the salad, combine all the ingredients together.

Slice the rested meat into pieces ½ inch thick and serve topped with the tuna sauce, fried capers, and the salad. This can be served warm, or at room temperature as part of a family-style feast.

TIP: *You want your veal to be blushing in the center, so it's best to give it plenty of time to rest before you carve it to prevent any wayward puddles of pink juice on your plate. The best thing to do is carve on a separate board to the one you'll serve from.*

THAI GREEN PAPAYA
SALAD WITH TROUT

Serves 4

The sight of a green papaya salad takes me to two places. In one, I'm sporting black cotton fisherman's pants I was certain were a good purchase at the time. I have a sunburn on my shoulders and I'm overlooking the turquoise waters of Kata Noi beach. In the second, I've been pregnant and bloated for 283 days, and am once again wearing those same pants (this time it's a choice determined by ease, not misguided elegance). Yet there's no reason to reserve the tingling enzymes of green papaya for Phuket or the very end of pregnancy (green papaya being an ingredient rumored to help bring on labor). The brilliant thing about these slender strands of unripe fruit, muddled with Thai basil, chili, and your choice of protein (I like trout, but shrimp, chicken, and duck are also great) is how light you'll feel after you've eaten them. Which means there's really no reason, bar comfort, to be swathing myself in loose, low-slung cotton pants, is there?

2¼ pounds green papaya (or green mango)
14 ounces cooked trout or shrimp, peeled (or poached,
   shredded chicken, or roasted, sliced duck)
½ cup roasted peanuts, roughly chopped
6 scallions, green bits shredded
14 ounces cherry tomatoes, halved
handful of fresh Thai basil leaves, torn

Dressing
1 large red chili, finely diced
2 garlic cloves, peeled and grated
1½ tablespoons palm sugar, grated or brown sugar
4 tablespoons lime juice
4 tablespoons fish sauce
1 tablespoon toasted sesame oil
3 teaspoons rice wine vinegar

To make the dressing, combine all the ingredients together and stir them until the sugar has dissolved.

Peel the skin from the papaya carefully. Use the shredding attachment on a mandoline to grate it, or cut it into sections and place them through the shredder of a food processor. If using a mango, be sure to avoid the seed.

Combine the salad ingredients with the dressing, reserving some of the peanuts to sprinkle on top.

CHICKEN
SAN CHOI BOW

Serves 4

To me san choi bow is often the opening salvo in a meal spun on a lazy susan, gluggy with rice and culminating in deep-fried ice cream. Yet there are plenty of ways to conjure the allure of a night at the local Chinese restaurant without installing a rotating circle in the middle of your dining table—or falling down a white carb hole. For one, leave the fried noodles, rice, and water chestnuts behind. Instead invite some slivered jicama/yam bean to the party. This bulbous root is often found in Asian grocery stores and has a similar texture to a water chestnut, but less bloating starch. From there you can pad out your lettuce packages with shaved carrot, ground meat, and the crunch of peanuts. And if you still feel the need for something white to spin on the table, take comfort in the fact you can always buy a rotating disk from IKEA.

1 large iceberg lettuce
2 teaspoons vegetable oil
5 scallions, thinly sliced
2 tablespoons chopped fresh cilantro stems
2-inch lump of ginger root, peeled and grated
1½ pounds ground chicken (or turkey or pork)
2 tablespoons light soy sauce
3 tablespoons hoisin sauce
1 tablespoon chili oil
1 teaspoon toasted sesame oil
½ jicama/yam bean (about 9 ounces), peeled and sliced
  on a mandoline, or 2 large handfuls of bean sprouts
1 carrot, peeled and grated
2 tablespoons roughly chopped roasted peanuts
2 tablespoons chopped fresh cilantro leaves

Cut the base from the iceberg lettuce and submerge in cold water to separate out the leaves. Trim them with scissors, if necessary, to make open cups. Place them in a bowl or sink of cold water to stay crisp.

Place a wok over high heat and add the vegetable oil. Stir-fry the scallions, cilantro stems, and ginger for 1 minute to soften them. Add the ground meat and cook for 4 to 6 minutes, until it takes on some color. Add the soy sauce, hoisin sauce, chili oil, and sesame oil.

Fold the stir-fry through the grated jicama/yam bean and carrot. Serve in the lettuce cups, top with the peanuts and cilantro leaves, and supply napkins to catch any drips.

PEPPERS STUFFED WITH CHIA, HUMMUS, AND PINE NUTS

Serves 2

Stuffed peppers aren't always the most appealing dish. In fact anyone who has ever dabbled with vegetarianism will probably have tasted some unspeakable versions, many of which more closely resemble miniature paddling pools than supper. The key is finding things to pad the center that won't leach excess liquid, leaving a soppy mess on your plate. Enter the chia seeds, which have a remarkable ability to absorb any surplus fluid. What follows is a pretty dish that's perfect for a summer mezze spread. Try coupling it with a very crisp green salad and some pickles if there are just two of you at the table, or combine it with the Smoky Eggplant with Tomatoes, Pickled Onion, Parsley, and Pomegranate Molasses (page 79) and some Quinoa and Zucchini Fritters with Strained Yogurt (page 40) and Roasted and Fresh Tomato Skewers with Mint and Halloumi (page 40) for a crowd.

7 ounces hummus
¼ cup chia seeds
1 tablespoon lemon juice
1 teaspoon ground cumin
½ teaspoon chili powder
1 red bell pepper, cut in half through the stem and seeded
2 tablespoons pine nuts
2 tablespoons olive oil

To serve
bitter greens and chili sauce

Preheat the oven to 350°F.

In a small bowl, mix together the hummus, chia seeds, lemon juice, and spices.

Portion the mixture into the cavities of the peppers. Top with the pine nuts and drizzle with the olive oil.

Put the peppers on a baking sheet and bake them in the preheated oven for 40 minutes, or until they have puckered around the edges and the pine nuts have lightly bronzed.

Serve the stuffed peppers on a bed of bitter greens, with chili sauce on the side.

FAVA BEAN, FENNEL, MINT, LEMON, AND PARMESAN SALAD

Serves 2

This is the kind of dish I make when there are clouds lazily bobbing across a blue sky and it's warm enough to roll your pants around your calves. It's a quick pull-together salad which also manages to look quite smart. Here are some other winning features: it takes just as much time to make as it does to soft-boil an egg. It's delicious with a sun-shiny yolk strewn over the top. It's also grand on its own as a side for barbecued chicken, shrimp, and both pink and white fish.

What you've got is a restrained balance of flavors—the mild anise of the fennel mellowed in olive oil, the sweetness of fava beans (frozen are fine—we've all got better things to do than pod beans), the richness of Parmesan, and a breath of fresh air from the mint and lemon.

If you haven't got a mandoline, I recommend using a vegetable peeler or the shaving attachment on your food processor to try and get the right sort of thickness in the fennel. Fat hunks just won't cut it here. If it's a big mouthful of anise you're after, you'd be better off munching some black licorice for dessert.

1 fennel bulb, finely shaved on a mandoline, with wafty green fennel tops set aside
7 ounces fresh or frozen fava beans (often available in Asian grocery stores)
grated zest and juice of ½ lemon
handful of fresh mint, finely chopped
1 ounce Parmesan, shaved
3 tablespoons olive oil
sea salt and freshly ground black pepper

Trim the bottom off the fennel. Put the mandoline on the slimmest setting you can get and carefully shave the fennel onto a plate.

If using frozen fava beans, gently steam them to defrost them.

Combine the fennel shavings, fennel tops, and beans with the lemon zest, the mint, and Parmesan. Season with salt and pepper.

Make a dressing by combining the olive oil and lemon juice, then drizzle it over the salad.

SORT-OF-WALDORF SALAD

Serves 2

The original version of this salad was first invented more than a century ago at the Waldorf Hotel. Celery, mayonnaise, apple, and walnuts were the key elements. These days I say you can keep your celery and wrinkled nuts along with your finery and napery. Here I've gone for fresh chunks of fennel and the crunch of almonds. For a dressing there's a lush slick of basil aïoli, though some basil leaves blended into thick Greek yogurt would suffice in a pinch. The only thing delicate here are some ribbons of mint, rolled up like a cigar and cut lengthwise, so they unfurl across the top of a salad like streamers. This is the sort of dish best enjoyed with a glass of chilled wine and possibly a bathrobe; not in a five-star hotel, but on your balcony at home.

3 cooked and cool or warm chicken thighs, cut into chunks the size of a wine cork (you could also use the meat off a store-bought barbecue chicken)
2 tablespoons basil aïoli (ie 2 teaspoons good-quality store-bought pesto mixed into 2 tablespoons good-quality mayonnaise)
1 fennel bulb, cut into small chunks
1 small Granny Smith apple, cored and cut into small chunks
½ avocado, pitted and diced
3 teaspoons slivered almonds, toasted
12 fresh mint leaves
sea salt and freshly ground black pepper

Combine the chicken with the basil aïoli, and fennel and apple chunks.

Gently add the avocado and sprinkle the almonds over the top.

Stack the mint leaves on top of each other. Roll them into a cigar widthwise and slice them thinly lengthwise to create little ribbons.

Add the mint ribbons to the salad and season with salt and pepper.

TIP: *Add the avocado just before serving. You want it to be fresh slivers of jade, not a sad mush of brown.*

TUNA NIÇOISE FISHCAKES

Makes 8 to 10 fishcakes, or serves 4
(and leftovers freeze well)

The fishcakes of my memories are leaden pucks of leftover mashed potato and flaked fish, often served with a limpid salad as an afterthought. This version is not only lighter, but breezier. The potato is replaced with white beans, which not only offer extra protein, but a nutty taste. The other flavors borrow heavily from the Provençal landscape of a Niçoise salad. Anchovies, capers, olives, and lemon all make cameos. I like to serve these fishcakes with a salad of green beans, olives, and blushingly ripe tomatoes drizzled with olive oil. If you feel like being slavishly devoted to the place of inspiration and can't find some nautical stripes to eat your dinner in, a soft-cooked egg relaxing over the top will help complete the picture.

2 x 14-ounce cans of white beans, rinsed
2 marinated anchovy fillets in olive oil, drained
grated zest and juice of 1 lemon
2 x 6½-ounce cans of solid-packed tuna, drained and flaked
1 egg, lightly beaten
1 tablespoon capers, diced
10 black olives, pitted and finely chopped
1 teaspoon freshly ground black pepper
3 tablespoons chickpea (besan or gram) flour

For dusting and frying
scant 1 cup chickpea (besan or gram) flour
sunflower or olive oil

To serve
a salad of steamed green beans, olives, chopped cherry
  tomatoes, and fresh basil leaves
lemon wedges

Blitz the white beans, anchovies, lemon zest, and juice together until smooth, using a stick blender or a food processor.

Add the tuna, beaten egg, capers, olives, pepper, and the 3 tablespoons chickpea flour to the mixture and stir to combine. Cover it and refrigerate for 1 hour if you have time—this will help the fishcakes to hold their shape.

When the mixture is ready to come out of the refrigerator, preheat the oven to 300°F.

Pour the scant 1 cup dusting flour onto a plate. Parcel out 3 tablespoons of the tuna mixture and shape between your hands to a disk about 3¼ inches across and ¾ inch high. Pat it in the flour until it's evenly coated all over. Repeat to form more patties with the remaining tuna mixture.

Pour enough oil in a large skillet to make a depth of ¹⁄₁₆ inch. Set it over medium heat and when the oil begins to shimmer, add the fishcakes in batches of 3 and fry them for 1 to 2 minutes on each side, or until crispy and golden. Keep the fishcakes hot in the oven while you fry the remaining batches.

Serve the fishcakes hot with a salad of green beans, olives, cherry tomatoes, and basil, and lemon wedges to squeeze over.

GRIDDLED CHILI PEPPERS STUFFED WITH FETA, BLACK BEANS, AND PUMPKIN SEEDS

Serves 2

The inspiration for this dish came initially from my stepbrother, a terrific cook in his own right, who one night for family dinner delivered from the barbecue a platter of blackened chili peppers stuffed with feta. It was an experiment that worked. This marries his thinking with a cleaner version of the Tex Mex classic of chiles rellenos omitting the battered crust and swapping the often greasy meat stuffing for rumpled black beans. The end result is a lovely light lunch when served with some guacamole on the side, and if you're in the mood, a margarita or two.

2–3 long red, banana chili peppers, split lengthwise, seeds and internal membranes scraped out
1 x 14-ounce can of black beans, rinsed and mashed with a potato masher (it can be rustic)
⅔ cup crumbled feta
3 tablespoons pumpkin seeds
handful of fresh cilantro leaves, chopped

To serve
1 lime
hot sauce
Guacamole (page 26)

To use a barbecue, preheat it to medium. Alternatively, use a griddle pan on the stove.

Stuff the chili peppers with the mashed black beans, then the feta.

Transfer the stuffed chili peppers to the barbecue or to a griddle pan and grill on each side (being careful that the stuffing doesn't fall out) for 4 minutes, or until the chili peppers are charred and blistered and the black beans have warmed through.

Top the chili peppers with the pumpkin seeds and cilantro. Serve with lime wedges, hot sauce, and guacamole.

SHRIMP, AVOCADO, AND EDAMAME SALAD

Serves 2

To me there's something quite meditative about popping these edamame (soybeans) out of their shells. If for some reason you need a bit of extra focus in your day, feel free to buy packs of frozen pods and pluck out the required beans one by one. For those who are doing just fine, many Asian grocery stores will sell frozen packs of edamame already shelled, like peas. In this salad they're combined with avocado, cucumber, green leaves, lime, and sesame, in what is essentially a zen take on shrimp cocktail.

7 ounces shelled edamame beans
2 handfuls of green leaves (a mix of baby spinach, watercress, and arugula is nice)
5-inch cucumber, shaved into ribbons with a vegetable peeler
7 ounces peeled, cooked shrimp (heads and digestive tracts removed)
1 lime (grated zest and juice of one half, and the other half cut into wedges)
1 teaspoon toasted sesame oil
1 tablespoon neutral-tasting oil
½ avocado, sliced
1½ teaspoon black sesame seeds (or toasted white sesame seeds)

Combine the edamame beans, green leaves, shaved cucumber, and shrimp. Add the lime zest.

Combine the lime juice with the oils and whisk to combine. Toss the dressing over the salad, then top with the avocado pieces and sesame seeds. Serve with the extra wedges of lime.

TIP: *I find it's best to gently place the avocado on the plate just before serving, to prevent it turning into unsightly mulch when you dress the salad. If you can't find edamame, feel free to substitute green peas, or fava beans.*

TANDOORI SALMON WITH SPICED LENTILS AND RAITA

Serves 4

This combination has swiftly become a midweek staple for not only our family, but a few of the testers who helped out in the production of this book. Why? Because it's aromatic but not too onerous and it easily halves or doubles, depending on how many are sitting at your table. But I think it's mainly because eating these yellow-hued lentils and rosy pink salmon makes us feel good, and not just because of the links between turmeric and reduced rates of cancer and dementia. Here are some tips: if you have the time, try to marinate your salmon for 30 minutes to help bed down the flavors. I do this while I'm making the lentils and setting the table. And be sure to include the sides of raita, fresh tomato, and a lemon wedge for squeezing—they really help to awaken the dish.

4 fillets of salmon (about 6½ ounces each), skin on
1 tablespoon olive oil
sea salt

Marinade
⅔ cup Greek yogurt
1 garlic clove, peeled and grated
¾-inch lump of ginger root, peeled and grated
1 teaspoon ground cumin
1 teaspoon ground turmeric
a pinch of sea salt
½ teaspoon freshly ground black pepper
1 teaspoon paprika
½–1 teaspoon cayenne pepper

Spiced lentils
1 tablespoon ground turmeric
1 teaspoon ground cumin
1 teaspoon cayenne pepper
1 teaspoon ground coriander
1 teaspoon ground cinnamon
1 teaspoon mustard seeds
1 tablespoon olive oil
1 onion, peeled and diced
2-inch lump of ginger root, peeled and grated
2 x 14-ounce cans of brown lentils, rinsed

Raita
1 small cucumber, grated and squeezed with your hands
  to remove excess moisture
small bunch of fresh mint, chopped
1¼ cups Greek yogurt

To serve
lemon wedges
handful of baby spinach
handful of cherry tomatoes, chopped

To make the marinade, combine all the ingredients together in a large bowl. Add the salmon fillets and coat the flesh in the marinade, leaving the skin clean. Cover and refrigerate for 30 minutes if you have time.

To make the spiced lentils, place all the spices in a skillet over medium heat and toast for 1 minute, or until they smell nutty. Add the olive oil, onion, and ginger and sauté for 3 to 5 minutes until the onion has softened, then tumble in the lentils and stir to warm them through.

To cook the salmon, take the fillets out of the marinade bowl and sprinkle the skin generously with salt to help stop it sticking to the pan. Heat the olive oil in a skillet over medium heat (or use a barbecue) and place the fillets, skin side down, in the pan. Cook for 3 minutes, then flip the fillets over and cook them for 2 to 3 minutes on the other side—most of the exterior of the salmon should be opaque except for about ½ inch halfway down. Inside, it will be gently blushing at its center, so if you prefer your salmon well done, cook it on the second side for an extra 2 minutes. Let the salmon rest for 2 to 3 minutes before serving.

To make the raita, combine the ingredients together.

Serve the salmon on the lentils with a lemon wedge for squeezing over the top, the spinach, cherry tomatoes, and the raita on the side.

MOROCCAN LAMB AND CHICKPEA BURGERS IN LETTUCE LEAVES

Makes 8 small burgers, or serves 4

Can you really get the joy of a burger without the bun? I hazard that with these, you can. It helps that there are smooshed beans in the patties, which are responsible for transforming this into a more sustaining supper than just mere meat and leaves. It's the kick of spices and sprightly mint-yogurt dressing which also completes their appeal. I like to eat these with some blistered tomatoes and a cool glass of pink wine, preferably with my toes dangling in a swimming pool.

9 ounces cherry tomatoes
2 tablespoons olive oil
1 x 14-ounce can of chickpeas, rinsed
2 garlic cloves, peeled and grated
1 tablespoon ground cumin
1 tablespoon ground coriander
1 teaspoon ground cinnamon
1 teaspoon ground ginger
½ teaspoon cayenne pepper
1 egg, lightly beaten
1½ teaspoons sea salt
1 pound 2 ounces ground lamb

Mint-yogurt dressing
⅔ cup Greek yogurt
handful of fresh mint leaves, torn
2 tablespoons olive oil

To serve
8 large leaves of soft lettuce
harissa or chili sauce

Preheat the oven to 300°F.

Put the tomatoes in a roasting tray, drizzle with half of the olive oil, and roast in the preheated oven for 40 minutes.

In the meantime, put three-quarters of the chickpeas, the garlic, spices, egg, and salt in a food processor and blitz to a paste.

Combine the chickpea paste with the ground lamb and remaining whole chickpeas. Divide the mixture into 8 portions and shape into fat disks between your hands. Put them on a plate, cover, and refrigerate for 15 to 30 minutes to firm up.

Heat the remaining olive oil in a skillet (or use a barbecue) over medium heat. Fry the burgers for 3 to 4 minutes on each side until the outside is burnished and the inside cooked medium–rare, if that's how you like it.

To make the mint-yogurt dressing, muddle all the ingredients together.

Serve the burgers in lettuce leaves with the roasted cherry tomatoes, mint-yogurt dressing, and harissa or chili sauce, to taste.

MEDITERRANEAN SQUID STUFFED WITH WHITE BEAN PURÉE AND OLIVES

Serves 2 generously

The immigration form to enter Malta lists eight check boxes of possible reasons for your visit. This is a problem. Not one of them mentions pastizzi. These small, brittle pastries stuffed with cheese became my undoing over three days on this island in the Mediterranean. That's until I discovered their version of braised octopus, stuffat tal-qarnit, cooked long and slow with tomatoes, olives, and onion. What follows is a meal which combines the flavors of that dish, with a little extra ballast. The cleaned squid tubes are chocked with cannellini beans and shrimp, bringing a double dose of the sea. You'll need some toothpicks to fasten the stuffed tubes closed and a little bit of dexterity. Hopefully this is a fish dish so satisfying you won't need to go in search of flaky pastries for a while, but if you're hankering for something sweet, try pairing it with the Baked Ricotta-Stuffed Peaches on page 162.

2 tablespoons olive oil

a pinch of crushed red pepper flakes

3 garlic cloves, peeled and sliced

1 onion, peeled and finely diced

4 medium or 8 small squid tubes (around 8 ounces in total), cleaned, plus tentacles set aside if you have them

1¾ cups strained tomatoes

1 x 14-ounce can of cannellini beans, drained

8 small, raw, peeled shrimp (1¾ cups), diced

2 handfuls of fresh flat-leaf parsley, chopped

10 black olives, pitted and finely chopped

To serve

salad of baby spinach leaves, shaved fennel, and shaved zucchini, dressed in olive oil and lemon juice

Equipment

8 toothpicks

Put the olive oil, red pepper flakes, garlic, and onion in a large heavy-bottom saucepan or Dutch oven over medium heat. Sauté for 5 to 7 minutes until the onion has softened. Add the squid tentacles if you have them and sauté until they tighten and take on a little color. Pour in the strained tomatoes and bring to a gentle simmer, then place the lid on the pan.

Prepare the filling for the squid. Mash the cannellini beans into a rustic paste. Stir in the shrimp, three-quarters of the parsley, and the olives.

Stuff the filling into the squid tubes, pushing it all the way down into the tips, and fasten the base with a toothpick.

Place the stuffed squids into the simmering tomato sauce. Place the lid back on and cook at a gentle simmer for 40 minutes—the squid should be opaque and the shrimp in the filling cooked through.

Serve the squid with the remaining parsley and the spinach, fennel, and zucchini salad.

PEACH PULLED PORK
WITH DIRTY QUINOA

Serves 4 to 6

Pulled pork should traditionally be eaten on a white roll so fluffy it could stand in for a duvet. What we need is something else to soak up the sticky juice and to act as a foil for the soft threads of meat. Dirty rice is one option. Cajun in origin, it traditionally melds the murk of chicken liver with rice. Here we can imitate its dark complexity with a few shades of quinoa, some lentils, and a hit of spice (though if you fancy adding in some ground chicken livers, go ahead). With the tacky sweetness of the peaches, this is a dish that cries out for some sharp cut-through—a slaw of cabbage dressed in apple cider vinegar would be one way, as would a piquant hot sauce. What is not negotiable is a napkin. This isn't clean eating, by any sense of the word.

1 tablespoon ground cumin

1 tablespoon ground coriander

1 teaspoon chili powder

½ tablespoon sea salt

grated zest and juice of 1 small orange

2¼ pounds well-marbled pork shoulder, cut into pieces the size of a matchbook

2 tablespoons olive oil

4 ripe peaches, pitted and chopped, or 7½ ounces drained canned peach halves

1⅔ cups ginger ale (or water)

sea salt

Dirty quinoa

scant ½ cup white quinoa, rinsed

scant ½ cup red or black quinoa, rinsed

1⅔ cups chicken stock

1 tablespoon ground cumin

1 x 14-ounce can of brown lentils, rinsed

handful of fresh cilantro, chopped

To serve

piquant hot sauce and/or cabbage slaw

Mix together the spices, ½ tablespoon salt, and the orange zest and tumble the pork pieces in it.

Heat the olive oil in a large, heavy-bottom saucepan or Dutch oven over high heat and add half the meat. Brown the meat all over, then remove it from the pan and do the same with the second half of the meat. Return all the meat to the pan with the orange juice and peaches. Add just enough ginger ale to cover the meat (topping off with water if you need more liquid). Bring the liquid to a rolling boil, then reduce it to a simmer and cook, uncovered, for 2 hours.

After 2 hours, check the meat. There should only be about a ¼-inch depth of liquid left in the pan and the meat should easily shred with 2 forks. Depending on the amount of marbling in the meat, it might need another 30 minutes or so.

About 20 minutes before serving, make the dirty quinoa. Put the quinoa, chicken stock, and cumin in a saucepan and bring it to a boil, then reduce the heat. Simmer with the lid on for 15 minutes, or until most of the liquid has been absorbed. Fold through the drained lentils, season with salt, and top with the cilantro.

When the pork is ready, shred it with 2 forks and toss it with the remaining juices.

Serve the pork with the dirty quinoa and some piquant hot sauce—and if you fancy, a slaw of shredded cabbage dressed with apple cider vinegar.

PIRI PIRI CHICKEN
WITH BLACK BEANS
AND TOMATOES

Serves 4 (with enough marinade
to freeze half for another time)

This could be a story about how when we went to Portugal we ate terrific piri piri chicken. Except it's not. Lisbon in late June is not for the fainthearted. It's searingly hot, the kind of heat where the sidewalk seems to warp from the beating beams of glare. The air is soupish and the only place you want to be is in the water, or the shade doing nothing more energetic than chasing stray drips off an ice cream. I'm sure if we looked properly we might have found the quarter of chicken, charred and blistered with peppers, oregano, citrus, and acids that we hoped for. Except we didn't. On our final day we resorted to eating salt cod with a side dish of mild disappointment. It wasn't until we returned home to London that I realized we didn't need to be in Portugal to have the chicken we dreamed of. All we needed were some spices, some patience—and a strong pair of scissors.

a 4–4½-pound chicken
9 ounces cherry tomatoes
2 x 14-ounce cans of black beans, rinsed
3 double handfuls of kale, roughly chopped
6 marinated red peppers, drained and diced
aïoli (page 42), to serve

Piri piri marinade
1 small red onion, peeled and cut into rough chunks
3 garlic cloves, peeled
½ cup olive oil
¼ cup red wine vinegar
1–2 chili peppers (seeded if you don't like things too spicy)
1 red bell pepper, seeded and roughly chopped
1 tablespoon paprika
½ tablespoon dried oregano
grated zest and juice of ½ lemon
a pinch of sea salt
crushed red pepper flakes or chili powder, to taste (optional)
brown sugar, to taste (optional)

Preheat the oven to 400°F.

To make the marinade, blitz all the ingredients together in a food processor until smooth. Taste and adjust the flavoring—if you like more heat, add red pepper flakes or some chili powder; if it's too acrid, add a little brown sugar. The sweetness and the heat will depend on which peppers, chili peppers, and red wine vinegar you use. You want a balance of warmth and vinegar.

Transfer the marinade to a skillet over medium heat and sauté it for 5 to 7 minutes to thicken it, stirring frequently. Set it aside to cool slightly.

To cut the backbone out of the chicken, the easiest method is with some kitchen scissors. Once it's been removed, splay the chicken out onto a board and press it down to flatten it. Pour half the marinade over the chicken and massage it into the skin. Set aside or freeze the other half of the marinade.

Place the chicken in a roasting tray with the cherry tomatoes. Bake it in the preheated oven for about 45 to 50 minutes, or until the chicken breast reaches 164°F internally and the juices in the leg of the chicken run clear when you prick it with a knife.

Let the chicken rest while you prepare the vegetables. Put the black beans, kale, roasted cherry tomatoes, and marinated peppers in a saucepan over medium heat and stir until the beans are warm and the kale has wilted.

Carve the chicken and serve it with the warmed vegetables, a little extra sauce from the roasting tray, and some aïoli on the side.

TIP: *It's well worth it to spatchcock the chicken. It allows the marinade to cover much more of the surface of the bird. It also allows the chicken to cook more swiftly.*

Is it possible to have comfort food with fewer carbs? Yes. It is. Whether it's gnocchi made from white beans, or the edible hug which is a blue cheese soufflé, all it takes is a few sneaky tricks here and there to turn the food that you crave on duvet days into stuff that still makes you feel good. Whether it's using chickpea flour in a béchamel, omitting the potatoes from your choucroute, or stuffing cabbage rolls with a combination of quinoa, ground meat, and mushrooms, there are plenty of ways to make your winter warmers a little lighter. This is the sort of food I want to make again and again when the wind is whipping and I'm searching for an excuse to turn the oven on. We'll raid the pantry and settle in with lentil meatballs with ajvar, or a lamb and fig tagine. We'll turn on the television. Occasionally we'll get to huddle by a fire. We may even get around to cracking a good bottle of red. Winter may be coming, but it doesn't have to be that bleak.

HUDDLE-BY-THE-FIRE COMFORT FOOD

BLUE CHEESE SOUFFLÉS

Serves 4

There is some unnecessary stigma surrounding soufflés. If you can make a white sauce and whip an egg white, you can make one. Sure there are some tips to ease the way—using room-temperature eggs will give a better rise, as will cooling the cheesy béchamel before you fold in the stiff whites. I tend to get the best results when I cook them on the lowest shelf of the oven (and then take them straight to the table, though don't fret too much, as it's in their nature to slouch when you serve them—a rumpled crown is part of the appeal). As light as the air is in these, the blue cheese makes them rather plush. Placing some plumes of radicchio on the side helps with cut-through, providing both a bitter contrast and an excellent device for dunking. I find one small portion of the soufflés is sufficient; any more can feel more onerous than indulgent. To round out the meal try serving them with the Chickpeas, Leek, Apple, and Pear Salad on page 75 for additional crunch and contrast.

1½ tablespoons butter, plus extra for greasing
2 tablespoons ground almonds or hazelnuts
⅓ cup chickpea (besan or gram) flour
1 cup milk
5 ounces blue cheese
½ tablespoon fresh thyme leaves
4 egg whites
sea salt and freshly ground black pepper
radicchio leaves, to serve

Equipment
4 x 9-ounce ramekins or small copper pots

Preheat the oven to 350°F.

Lightly grease the ramekins or copper pots with butter. Pour the ground nuts into the base of one and shake it to coat the sides with the nuts, then pour the excess into the next ramekin or pot and repeat until they have all been dusted.

Place a saucepan over medium heat. Add the butter and let it melt, then add the flour and stir it to create a paste. Cook the paste for 2 minutes, or until it has turned a light brown.

Gradually pour in the milk, whisking it with a balloon whisk until it thickens to a gloopy white sauce like béchamel. Add the cheese and thyme and stir until the cheese has melted and the mixture is smooth. Remove the pan from the heat, season the mixture with salt and pepper, and let it cool for at least 5 minutes.

In a clean bowl, use an electric whisk to beat the egg whites with a pinch of salt until soft peaks form. Fold the egg whites into the cheese mixture in 3 batches, trying not to knock too much air out, until everything is just combined.

Portion the soufflé batter into the prepared ramekins or pots, filling them just three-quarters full, and place them on a baking sheet on the bottom shelf of the preheated oven. Bake them for 25 minutes until puffed up and golden brown.

Serve the soufflés immediately with radicchio leaves for dipping, and potentially the Chickpeas, Leek, Apple, and Pear Salad on page 75.

TIP: *You could easily substitute the blue cheese for crumbled goat cheese or gratings of a good cheddar. If you're looking for a way to use up your leftover egg yolks, try the passionfruit curd on page 161, perhaps substituting the zest and juice of a clementine to give it a wintry twist. The curd is lovely layered with yogurt as a light dessert.*

BAKED WHITE-BEAN GNOCCHI WITH MEATBALLS, MOZZARELLA, AND TOMATO

Serves 2

To me, potato gnocchi are the greatest comfort food of all, and one of the things I was saddest to let go of when I tried to curb my carb addiction. Then I began musing—is it possible to make gnocchi from beans?

The answer is yes. And while purists may roll their eyes, it has the added benefit of being the quickest and easiest gnocchi I've ever made. It's two cans of white beans, drained and rinsed, then blitzed with a stick blender. That's something you can't do with potatoes, unless you want to use the resulting purée to hold up wallpaper. If I'm craving really fluffy gnocchi I'll work the purée through a strainer or a mouli. This helps get out all errant lumps and incorporate as much air as possible. I'll acknowledge, this isn't completely carb-free, but it's not the double excesses of potato and flour that you'll find in the original. The extra protein in the beans will make them a little sturdier than potato gnocchi, but when baked they possess a very pleasing contrast of external crunch to inside squish.

sea salt and freshly ground black pepper

Gnocchi
2 x 14-ounce cans lima or cannellini beans, rinsed
   (leaving 3 cups beans when drained)
1 egg yolk
¾ cup all-purpose or "00" white wheat flour, plus extra for
   dusting
olive oil, for drizzling

Sauce
11 ounces cherry tomatoes
1 tablespoon olive oil
7 ounces ground beef or pork
1 teaspoon dried oregano
3 tablespoons tomato paste (more if the tomatoes aren't as
   juicy as you hoped)
a pinch of sugar
11 ounces buffalo mozzarella, roughly torn
fresh basil or oregano leaves, to garnish

Equipment
baking sheet lined with parchment paper
ovenproof dish, the size of an A4 sheet of paper

Preheat the oven to 350°F. For the gnocchi, purée the beans using a stick blender or food processor until completely smooth. For the best results, pass the purée through a strainer or mouli. Put the purée, egg yolk, and a good pinch of salt in a large bowl. Sift the flour in, bit by bit, and use one hand to lightly and gently bring it together into a dough. Don't work it too hard otherwise it will become tough.

Dust a clean bench with a little more flour. Divide the dough into 4 balls. Hold your hands out, flat, on top of one portion of dough. Press it as though you were pushing a piece of paper away from you and then pulling it back toward you to roll the dough into a long rope as thick as a wine cork. Set it aside and repeat with the remaining 3 balls of dough.

Line the dough ropes up next to each other and simultaneously cut all 4 into gnocchi around ⅝ inch long. (Lining the ropes up next to each other will help create equal-sized gnocchi.) Place the gnocchi on the lined baking sheet, drizzle lightly with olive oil, and bake in the preheated oven for 20 minutes. This helps the gnocchi to set so they don't get too slimy when they are baked in the sauce later on.

Reduce the oven temperature to 300°F. For the sauce, put the cherry tomatoes in the ovenproof dish, drizzle with the olive oil, and sprinkle with a pinch of salt. Bake in the oven for 20 minutes, or until the tomatoes have softened and wrinkled.

While the tomatoes are roasting, make the meatballs. Combine the meat with the dried oregano, a pinch of salt, a good grinding of black pepper, and 1 tablespoon of very cold water. Squash it all together with your hands, and then portion the mixture into meatballs the same size as the cherry tomatoes. When the tomatoes have been in the oven for 20 minutes, add the meatballs to the dish and pop the dish back in the oven for another 20 minutes.

When the tomatoes are roasted, bloated, and softened from the oven, squash them with a fork to encourage the innards to ooze out and make a sauce. Add the tomato paste and sugar and stir gently. Nestle the gnocchi in among the meatballs and the tomatoes. You want to make sure that there is enough liquid from the busted tomatoes to come at least halfway up the sides of the gnocchi. If not, add another 1–2 tablespoons tomato paste muddled with a little water, or make up the shortfall with strained tomatoes.

Top with the well-drained and torn mozzarella and bake for 30 minutes, or until the cheese has melted and browned and the gnocchi are cooked through.

Serve the baked gnocchi with basil or oregano on top.

CHOUCROUTE

Serves 6

An Alsatian specialty involving the tang of sauerkraut and the smoky intensity of pork, choucroute is often served with potatoes. I first realized that they were extraneous to the experience beneath the vaulted ceiling of London's The Delaunay. I was more than happy to leave my perfectly turned tubers to the side to save room for a slice of torte. Since that day, I've never missed them. At the outset, choucroute may seem involved, but it's really more of an assembly job, since the sauerkraut and sausages come ready formed. Be sure not to omit the apples and juniper berries— they provide the necessary floral notes to balance the acidity of the cabbage. Beyond that, a variety of mustards on the table to share will help pull the fattiness of the pork into line. Add a lager or two, or a nice bottle of Riesling, and you've got the makings of a proper celebration. (And if you're looking for a fitting treat with which to finish the meal, try the Salzburger Nockerl on page 158 or the Black Forest notes of the Chocolate, Black Bean, and Cherry Cake on page 164).

1½ pounds sauerkraut in brine
1 tablespoon olive oil
1¾ pounds good-quality pork sausages
3 onions, peeled and diced
2 medium carrots, peeled and diced
1 garlic clove, peeled and grated
2 green apples, peeled, cored, and grated
1⅔ cups chicken stock
generous 2 cups dry white wine (Riesling is classic)
1 fresh or dried bay leaf
6 black peppercorns
6 cloves
8 juniper berries
7 ounces thick-cut ham steaks, cut into pieces the size
  of a matchbox
14 ounces smoked sausage (try kielbasa, cabanossi,
  bratwurst)

To serve
Dijon mustard, whole grain mustard, and German mustard

Rinse the sauerkraut from its brine and set it aside to drain.

Preheat the oven to 325°F.

Put the olive oil in a large, ovenproof Dutch oven over medium heat and add the pork sausages. Stir them until they are evenly browned, then remove them from the dish and set them aside.

In the same dish, sauté the onions and carrots for 5 to 7 minutes until they have softened. Add the garlic and apples and stir for 2 minutes. Add the sauerkraut, stock, wine, bay leaf, peppercorns, cloves, and juniper berries and bring to a simmer.

Return the browned sausages to the dish, place the lid on, and bake in the preheated oven for 1½ hours.

Tuck the cut ham and smoked sausage into the Dutch oven and replace the lid. Return to the oven and bake for another 30 minutes, or until the meats have heated through. Pluck out the bay leaf, warn your guests about the juniper berries and peppercorns, and serve the choucroute with the mustards.

EGGPLANT "PARM"

Serves 4 (or 6 with a big green salad,
or as a side for some roast lamb, steak, or fish)

*This dish is half a meatless moussaka and half a pimped
up "parm." It's also one with some secrets buried
inside. It's up to you whether you want to let people in
on the fact that the béchamel is bolstered by a can of
blitzed cannellini beans and an egg. They'll probably
never know they're there but you'll appreciate the
extra protein. The second is the use of a panini press
to toast your eggplant slices. It saves on oil from frying
(eggplants can be the thirstiest of nightshades) and
thanks to the heat coming from both sides it will cook
them in double time. There's a little bit of hands-on
work in layering it all together, but the end result is
something that's hearty, bubbling, and very hard to
just have one portion of.*

3 large eggplants
3 tablespoons olive oil
3¼ ounces Parmesan, shaved
5 ounces mozzarella
large handful of fresh basil leaves, to serve
sea salt and freshly ground black pepper

Tomato sauce
1 tablespoon olive oil
1 onion, peeled and diced
2 garlic cloves, peeled and thinly sliced
2 x 14-ounce cans of chopped tomatoes
1 tablespoon dried oregano
a pinch of crushed red pepper flakes (optional)

Béchamel
2 tablespoons butter
scant ½ cup chickpea (besan or gram) flour or
  all-purpose flour
1¾ cups milk
1 x 14-ounce can of cannellini beans or chickpeas rinsed and
  puréed (to help create a smoother purée you can add
  2 tablespoons milk or water)
1 egg, lightly beaten

Equipment
lasagna dish, 12 inches long, greased

Lop the top off the eggplants. Cut them lengthwise into
slices ⅝ inch thick and brush them with the olive oil.

Use a panini press or a griddle pan to "toast" the
eggplant slices in batches, until the outsides are golden
brown and the insides are pliable.

Meanwhile, to make the tomato sauce, heat the olive oil
in a skillet over medium heat and sauté the onion and
garlic for 5 to 7 minutes until they have softened, taking
care not to scorch the garlic. Add the canned tomatoes,
oregano, and red pepper flakes and bring it to a simmer.
You want the sauce to cook until it is thick and chunky.
Taste it: if it is a little acrid, add a teaspoon of sugar.
Now is also the time to add salt to taste.

Preheat the oven to 350°F.

While the tomato sauce is reducing, take a separate
saucepan and make the béchamel. Melt the butter
over medium heat, then add the flour and stir it to
create a paste. Cook the paste for 2 minutes, or until
it has turned a light brown. Gradually pour in the milk,
whisking it with a balloon whisk until it thickens to
a nice, lump-free white sauce like béchamel. Stir in
the puréed beans, then remove from the heat and
stir through the egg and ½ teaspoon pepper.

Lay one-third of the grilled eggplants across the bottom
of the prepared lasagna dish, top to tail to help fill all
the corners. It can be quite rustic. Cover them with
half the tomato sauce and one-third of the Parmesan
and mozzarella. Layer another third of the eggplants,
then cover them with the remaining tomato sauce
and another third of the cheeses. Use the remaining
eggplants to form a final layer.

Pour the béchamel evenly over the top, making sure
to leave a few inches clear at the top of the dish
as the sauce will rise a little with baking. Sprinkle with
the remaining cheeses.

Bake the "parm" in the preheated oven for 45 minutes,
or until the top is golden and bubbling.

Serve strewn with basil leaves.

LAMB SHANK AND FIG TAGINE

Serves 4 to 6

Most of the tagines I ate in Marrakech were elegant trios—lamb, prune, and onion, or chicken, peppers, and lemon—and yet they fell flat. It may have been the heat. Stewed meats are just not what I fancy when the mercury is tipping 104˚ F. What follows is by no means a muffled braise, but a busy jumble of spices and textures. And to me this aromatic combination of slow-cooked lamb and vegetables has swiftly become the perfect wintry Sunday night supper. It's self-contained enough to justify pulling the slow cooker down from the top of the cupboard, or dusting off the Dutch oven. I find that the chickpeas bobbing about in here are perfectly filling and all I need is a splash of yogurt and a dab of harissa to make it sing. If you really crave something strapping as a base, try it with some quinoa or some plain Cauliflower "Couscous" from page 76.

3 tablespoons olive oil
4 large or 6 medium lamb shanks (or 2¼ pounds diced lamb
    shoulder, chicken thighs, or peeled sweet potato)
2 teaspoons sea salt
2 onions, peeled, halved, and cut into slim half-moons
2 carrots, peeled and sliced
2 garlic cloves, peeled and sliced
1 teaspoon ground cumin
1 teaspoon ground coriander
1 teaspoon ground ginger
1 teaspoon ground cinnamon
a pinch of chili powder
3 cups chicken stock
a pinch of saffron threads
1 x 14-ounce can of chickpeas, rinsed
7 ounces dried figs, cut in half

To serve
plain yogurt
fresh cilantro
harissa or chili sauce, to taste
quinoa or Cauliflower "Couscous" (see page 76) (optional)

Preheat the oven to 300˚F.

Put 2 tablespoons of the olive oil in an ovenproof Dutch oven over medium heat. Season the lamb shanks with the salt and add them, in batches, to the Dutch oven to sear them. Be careful not to overcrowd the pan. Sear them until they are evenly browned, then remove them from the dish and set them aside.

Add the remaining olive oil to the Dutch oven and sauté the onions, carrots, garlic, and spices (bar the saffron) for 5 to 7 minutes until the vegetables have begun to soften and the spices smell toasty.

Pour the chicken stock into the dish and scrape the bottom with a metal spoon to rescue any flavor that's clinging to the pot. Add the saffron, chickpeas, figs, and lamb shanks, then bring the stock to a simmer. Clamp on a lid and cook in the preheated oven for 3 to 4 hours, until the meat is slinking off the bone and the figs are nice and soft.

Serve the tagine with yogurt, fresh cilantro, chili sauce, and quinoa or Cauliflower "Couscous," if you need some additional fodder.

PORK, BEEF, AND MUSHROOM-STUFFED CABBAGE ROLLS

Serves 4

When I married into a surname comprised of a smash of consonants, it carried with it a new world of foods. Cabbage rolls were the first through the door. They're a prized dish from the Romanian/Croatian arm of the family, and one of my husband's favorite childhood comfort foods. He first converted me to their charm by describing them as carbless cannelloni. It's half right. The Haschka family's version is made from home-pickled cabbage which sheaths a bundle of paprika-spiced ground meat and rice. It's the sort of food which encourages you to stand up straight and face the day with confidence. This version takes a shortcut by skipping the pickling, instead wilting the cabbage under hot water. There's also the nuttiness of quinoa in place of white rice, and some additional earthiness from the mushrooms. You can easily use ground veal for the pork, or go completely vegetarian and triple the quantity of mushrooms. We serve it with some sauerkraut for an acidic kick and a slick of sour cream or yogurt for a bit of extra richness. I haven't quite mustered the courage to make this version for the extended family and experts yet, but one day, maybe I will.

1 whole head of savoy cabbage
1 tablespoon olive oil
7 ounces white mushrooms, thinly sliced
1 tablespoon fresh thyme leaves
5 ounces ground pork
5 ounces ground beef
1½ tablespoons paprika
1 tablespoon fresh flat-leaf parsley, chopped
2 garlic cloves, peeled and finely chopped
1 cup cooked quinoa
1 x 24-ounce can of strained tomatoes
sea salt and freshly ground black pepper

To serve
sauerkraut and crème fraîche or sour cream

Preheat the oven to 350°F and boil some water.

Cut the base from the cabbage, submerge in cold water, and pull the outer leaves off, one by one. Place the leaves in a large saucepan and pour the boiling water over them. Let them soak for 2 minutes to soften, then refresh them under cold water.

Put the olive oil in a saucepan over medium heat and sauté the mushrooms and thyme until the mushrooms have browned. Let cool.

Mix together the meats, 1 tablespoon of the paprika, the parsley, garlic, and cooled mushrooms and thyme. Season well with salt and pepper. Fold through the cooked quinoa and mix well to combine.

Pour half the strained tomatoes into a Dutch oven and set aside.

To assemble the cabbage rolls, first cut out and discard the tough stem from the centre of the blanched cabbage leaves.

Place 1½–2 tablespoons of the filling in the center of each leaf. Roll the top of the leaf down over the filling, then tuck in the 2 sides and continue rolling until you have a neat little package. Set the roll aside, seam side down, and repeat the process with the remaining leaves and filling.

Nestle the rolls, seam side down, on the tomatoes in the Dutch oven. Pour the remaining tomatoes over the top and sprinkle with the remaining paprika. Place the lid on the dish and bake in the preheated oven for 1 hour.

After 1 hour, remove the lid and bake for another 30 minutes to help the sauce to reduce and thicken.

Serve the cabbage rolls with sauerkraut and a splash of crème fraîche or sour cream.

LENTIL "MEATBALLS" WITH AJVAR AND TOMATO

Makes 14 to 16 "meatballs,"
or serves 2 generously, or 4 with a large salad

Ajvar is a Balkan secret weapon in the kitchen. It's a robust relish made from roasted peppers and garlic. Its piquancy makes it perfect with grilled meats— most often we've enjoyed it on the side of a simple mixed grill. I'm happy to report that it also makes a novel sauce for "meatballs." These small spheres of lentils are an excellent stand-in on Meatless Mondays —and filling enough for you to easily forgo any pasta or mashed potato as a base. Just add some flat-leaf parsley and a little sour cream to the top before serving, though a big green salad and some pickles on the side are also great.

2 x 14-ounce cans of brown lentils, rinsed
2 tablespoons finely grated Parmesan
1 tablespoon tomato paste
1 egg, lightly beaten
2 tablespoons fresh flat-leaf parsley, finely chopped,
    plus extra to serve
1 tablespoon Hungarian paprika
a pinch of sea salt
chickpea (besan or gram) or whole wheat flour (optional)
2 tablespoons olive oil

Sauce
19-ounce ajvar (Balkan red pepper relish)
7 ounces cherry tomatoes

To serve
4 tablespoons crème fraîche or sour cream
green salad
pickles

Equipment
baking sheet lined with parchment paper

Using a stick blender or food processor, blend four-fifths of the lentils until smooth. Fold in the remaining lentils, the Parmesan, tomato paste, egg, parsley, paprika, and salt. The mixture should hold together like cookie dough but if it is too wet and droopy, you can rescue it by adding 1–2 tablespoons chickpea or whole wheat flour. Portion the mixture into meatballs the same size as golf balls. They will get a little mucky. Place them on the lined baking sheet and refrigerate them for 30 minutes to firm up.

Preheat the oven to 350°F.

After 30 minutes, drizzle the meatballs with the olive oil and transfer the baking sheet to the preheated oven. Bake for 25 to 30 minutes until they have browned.

In the meantime, for the sauce, put the ajvar and tomatoes in a saucepan over medium heat until the tomatoes have softened and popped and the ajvar has heated through.

Serve the meatballs on the sauce, glossed with a little crème fraîche or sour cream and some parsley. Eat with a green salad and some pickles on the side.

TIP: *Ajvar is available in the international foods section of many grocery stores. Otherwise you can fashion your own by blending together an 18-ounce jar of drained roasted red peppers with a garlic clove, 2 teaspoons olive oil, and 1 teaspoon red wine vinegar.*

THYME-ROASTED CHICKEN LEGS WITH BRAISED BABY LETTUCE AND PEAS

Serves 2 generously

This is not so much a recipe as a formula for dinner-party success, even if what you're hosting is just an intimate meal for two. One of the most sympathetic and indestructible pieces of meat to cook is a chicken leg with the thigh still attached. Here you get the perfect mix of crisp skin and dark meat without the hassle of trying to carve a bird in front of company. All you need to do is season them and shut the oven for 40 minutes and they'll be golden every time. What you want then is a low-maintenance side dish that does most of its work in tandem. The answer lies in a tasty trivet. This base of flavors will benefit from the roasting juices that seep down from the bird, while helping to lift it up. To me the combination of bacon, onion, and garlic are perfect. While the legs are resting, that trio becomes the backbone of a French-accented dish of peas with sweet braised and shredded lettuce. It's a tactic that travels well. If it's Spain that beckons, replace the bacon with chorizo and throw some cherry tomatoes and smoked paprika in with the greens. If it's Italy, then switch the thyme for oregano and use Tuscan kale instead of lettuce. And if it's more of an Asian sojourn you're after, then lob in some lap cheong (Chinese sausage) for bacon and put into play some wilted Chinese greens.

3¼ ounces bacon pieces or smoked bacon, finely chopped
2 small–medium onions, peeled, halved, and sliced
  into half-moons
3 garlic cloves, peeled and grated
2 chicken leg and thigh joints
2 teaspoons fresh thyme leaves
1 teaspoon sea salt flakes
Dijon mustard, to serve

Braised lettuce and peas
2 Boston lettuces, cored and very finely shredded
2¼ cups frozen peas
½ cup white wine

Preheat the oven to 350°F.

Line a baking sheet with the bacon, onions, and garlic—this is the "trivet" that forms the base of the dish and provides all the flavor. Sprinkle the top of the chicken legs with the thyme and salt, then place them on the trivet in the baking sheet. Bake in the preheated oven for 40 minutes, or until the juices from the thigh joint run clear.

Remove the chicken from the baking sheet and set it aside somewhere warm to rest.

For the braised lettuce and peas, transfer the trivet and all the chicken juices to a large saucepan or Dutch oven over high heat and fry to ensure all the fat on the bacon has rendered. Add the lettuce, peas, and wine and braise over medium heat until the lettuce has wilted and the peas are warmed through.

Serve the chicken over the braised lettuce and peas with a dab of Dijon mustard.

TIP: *It should go without saying that in all of this, buying cage-range and organic chicken legs will make all the difference to the end result.*

SHRIMP AND QUINOA GRITS

Serves 2 generously

Shrimp cooked in bacon grease and bobbing across a lake of grits is about as Southern as y'all can get. These puddles of hominy are almost a kissing cousin of semolina and cornmeal and the true definition of rib-sticking sustenance. Yet if it's treated with a little extra love and attention, you can get a similar squelching appeal (but lighter effect) from gussied-up quinoa. Gloss it with a little cream cheese for ooze and add in some lemon zest for lift. If you cook the quinoa in chicken stock it will also help boost the flavors— though if you're after an extra kick, try roasting the shells of your shrimp for 15 minutes in a moderate oven and infusing them in the warm chicken stock for 20 minutes. This may be a classic breakfast during a Southern summer when shrimp are in season but I find it's also a heartwarming dinner in winter— and a great way to revive any crustaceans you've stashed in the freezer.

1 cup quinoa, rinsed
generous 2 cups chicken stock
2 tablespoons cream cheese
½ lemon
1 tablespoon butter
1 tablespoon olive oil
1 red chili, finely chopped
6 scallions, white and green bits finely chopped
2 garlic cloves, peeled and thinly sliced
3½ ounces (2 slices) smoked bacon, cut into small sticks
1 pound 2 ounces raw shrimp, peeled, and heads and
　digestive tracts removed (11 ounces peeled weight)
piquant hot sauce, to serve (optional)

Put the quinoa and chicken stock in a saucepan and bring it to a boil, then reduce the heat. Simmer with the lid on for 15 minutes, or until most of the liquid has been absorbed. Stir through the cream cheese, and grate in the zest from the lemon half (and then set aside the lemon half). You want a slightly droopy consistency, so if it is too tight, add more cream cheese or a slosh of hot water.

While the quinoa is cooking, put a large skillet over medium heat and add the butter, olive oil, half of the chili, white bits of the scallions, garlic, and bacon. Add the reserved lemon half, cut side down, in the pan. Cook until the bacon has begun to render its fat and take on some color.

Add the shrimp and cook for 3 to 4 minutes until they have turned nicely pink. Remove them from the pan.

Squeeze the burnished lemon into the pan and scrape up any color that has clung to the bottom to create a rustic sauce. Serve the shrimp over the quinoa, topped with the bacon and pan juices. Top with the remaining chili, the piquant hot sauce, if you like, and a handful of the green bits from the scallions.

SAUSAGES WITH LEEKS, CARAMELIZED ONIONS, MUSHROOMS, AND BEANS

Serves 4

This is a dish borne from a frosty afternoon of refrigerator foraging. Sausages, onion, leek, and mushrooms were what were left in the kitchen one day when Baby Will was just three weeks old. I couldn't bring myself to drag the pram outside into the cold to fetch anything more. I was also hunting for any excuse to turn the oven on to steal some chill from the air. It turned into the happiest of coincidences. By baking the sausages and mushrooms I ended up with crisp edges to contrast with the silky softness of the leeks and the onions, while the creamed beans tied it all together. The end result is a perfectly homely dish, best consumed from bowls on the sofa, while a wee one who's wrapped up in a bunny rug snuffles and grunts like an old man beside you.

9 ounces white mushrooms, halved
14 ounces small pork or beef sausages
3 tablespoons olive oil
1 red onion, peeled, halved, and cut into slim half-moons
1 leek, green parts trimmed and discarded, remainder rinsed and sliced into coins ¼ inch thick
½ cup water
1 teaspoon Dijon mustard
2 x 14-ounce cans of cannellini beans, rinsed
1 teaspoon grated nutmeg
2 handfuls of baby spinach
sea salt and freshly ground black pepper
3 tablespoons crème fraîche, to serve

Preheat the oven to 350°F.

Put the mushrooms and sausages in a large ovenproof Dutch oven, drizzle with 1 tablespoon of the olive oil, and bake in the preheated oven for about 30 minutes.

In the meantime, put the remaining olive oil in a skillet over medium heat and sauté the onion and leek for 20 minutes, stirring occasionally, until they have softened and taken on a golden hue.

Using a stick blender or food processor, blitz together the water, mustard, and 1 can of the beans until you have a smooth purée.

Add the softened onion and leek, roasted mushrooms and sausages, second can of beans, bean purée, nutmeg, and spinach into the Dutch oven and place on the stove over low heat until the spinach wilts. Season with salt and pepper to taste and top with the crème fraîche before serving.

MISO EGGPLANT WITH GINGER TOFU AND ADZUKI BEANS

Serves 2 to 3

The appeal of nasu dengaku is largely textural: it's hard to turn away from a plinth of scored eggplant capped with a glaze of sticky miso. What it needs to transform it from a winning snack to a proper meal is some substance. Enter adzuki beans. Adzuki beans may physically resemble black beans, but their taste is milder and naturally sweeter. Cook them in the same pot in which you made your glaze and you'll end up with a terrific tumble of taste and texture. I find if I add a small rectangle of broiled tofu and a salad of raw snow peas and cucumber dressed with yuzu, I've got all bases covered. Remember, the joy of miso paste is that it's already fermented and won't go off, so it's well worth keeping some tucked in the refrigerator in a Tupperware for when you need a quick meal.

2 medium or 1 large eggplant
2 tablespoons neutral-tasting oil
5 tablespoons white (shiro) miso
¾-inch lump of ginger root, peeled and grated
1 teaspoon toasted sesame oil
2 teaspoons brown sugar
4 tablespoons mirin rice wine
1 x 14-ounce can of adzuki beans, rinsed
7 ounces firm tofu, drained and cut into 2 steaks
2 scallions, white and green bits finely chopped
1 tablespoon black sesame seeds
salad of raw snow peas and cucumber, to serve

Preheat the oven to 400°F.

Lop the tops off the eggplants, then cut them into thirds, lengthwise. Score the eggplant slices a few times with the tip of a sharp knife, taking care not to cut all the way through to the bottom. Brush them with the neutral-tasting oil and place them on a baking sheet. Roast them in the preheated oven for 35 to 40 minutes, until the slices are tender when pierced.

While the eggplants are roasting, put the miso, ginger, sesame oil, sugar, and 3 tablespoons of the mirin in a saucepan over medium heat. Whisk to combine and let it warm up.

When the eggplants are ready, switch the oven over to broiler mode and turn it up to high.

Paint the scored tops of the eggplant slices with the miso mixture and put them back on the baking sheet. Add the beans to the pan you made the miso mixture in and warm them over low heat.

Nestle the tofu slices in and around the eggplant slices on the sheet and drizzle them with the remaining mirin. Top with the white bits of the scallions. Place the sheet under the broiler and broil until the miso topping is bronzed and bubbling and the tofu is lightly tanned.

Serve the broiled tofu and eggplant on the beans and topped with the sesame seeds and the green bits of the scallions. Accompany with a snow pea and cucumber salad.

TIP: *For this dish, be sure to have the palest "shiro"/ white miso you can find. The regular brown miso will be too savory for the right balance of flavors here.*

DUCK BREASTS WITH ROAST BEET, RADISH, AND COCOA

Serves 4

Apart from their unique ability to stain everything in the kitchen when peeled, beet are special things. When roasted in their skins, protected under a canopy of foil, they become lollipop sweet. On their own they'd be fine. But believe me when I say the mild bitterness of a puckered radish and a grating of dark chocolate really make them shine. Beets and cocoa have long been friends—the internet is teeming with accounts of their joint escapades in brownies, whoopie pies, and cake pops. Here the darkest chocolate adds some murky intrigue to a warm salad which becomes festively fabulous with duck breasts—and for those in the southern hemisphere it will do the same for char-grilled fillets of kangaroo. Either way, you've got a feast that's worth risking a little bit of tainted skin for.

bunch of fresh, medium beets (about 10 in total)—
   it's lovely if you can get varying colors
bunch of radishes (about 10 in total)
2 tablespoons olive oil
1 tablespoon salt
¾ ounce very dark chocolate (minimum 70% cocoa solids,
   but 85–90% is best), finely grated
4 medium duck breasts, skin on and trimmed of sinew
2 tablespoons blanched hazelnuts, toasted
sea salt and freshly ground black pepper

Preheat the oven to 400°F.

Wash the beets and radishes to remove any dirt and trim the stalks to leave a few inches tufting out of the top. Take 2 radishes, shave them into slivers on a mandoline or with a vegetable peeler, and put them in a bowl of cold water to stay crisp.

You want all the beets and remaining radishes to be around the same size. If some are much bigger, cut them in half to ensure a more even cooking time. Aim for no larger than a golf ball. Scatter them on a baking sheet.

Drizzle the beets and radishes with the olive oil and season with 1 tablespoon salt. Cover the sheet with foil and bake in the preheated oven for 1½ to 2 hours until a skewer easily slides through the center.

When the vegetables are done, remove them from the oven and leave the oven on. Let the vegetables cool slightly, then rub the skins off the beets—it's best to wear rubber gloves when you do this!

Sprinkle the chocolate over the top of the roasted vegetables. Season with a little extra salt and pepper.

Score lines in the skin of the duck breasts using a small, sharp knife, being careful not to cut all the way through to the flesh underneath. Season the scored skin with salt. Place 2 duck breasts, skin side down, in a cold skillet and set over the highest heat. When you hear the fat start to sizzle, cook for 4 minutes. Remove them from the pan, set aside, clean out the pan, and repeat the cooking process with the other 2 duck breasts.

Transfer all the duck breasts to the oven and cook for 5 minutes for rare, and 8 minutes or longer if you like things cooked through.

Let the duck rest for 5 minutes before carving it into thick slices. Serve with the roasted vegetables, toasted hazelnuts, and raw radish slivers.

WHITE-BEAN COLCANNON WITH STICKY BRAISED BEEF

Serves 4 to 6 with a salad

Trying to win some friends over to a spudless way of eating can be hard going. You may struggle to convince a Dubliner that a colcannon made from white beans is worth their time. But the humble cabbage—in this case the deep emerald hues of kale—has proved it can still be a star when folded through any mass of mash, whether potato or bean. This version of colcannon is an excellent complement for many family basics; from sausages with slow-cooked onion gravy, pork chops with apple sauce to sticky slow-cooked beef stews. This braised beef is a no-fuss sort of supper. Start the stew in the morning and let it blip away all afternoon. The end result is bold and confident, calming, and comforting all at once.

sea salt and freshly ground black pepper

Sticky braised beef

2 tablespoons olive oil

5 ounces small bacon pieces or bacon cut into slim strips

2¼ pounds chuck steak or beef shin with a good amount of white sinew marbled through, cut into ¾-inch cubes (avoid a lean cut as it will turn to leather over long cooking)

3 medium carrots, peeled, halved lengthwise, and cut into ½-inch thick slices

2 onions, peeled, halved, and cut into slim half-moons

11 ounces white mushrooms, halved

3 garlic cloves, peeled and finely diced

generous 2 cups beef stock

3 tablespoons Worcestershire sauce

White-bean colcannon

2 x 14-ounce cans of white beans, rinsed

2 tablespoons milk

3½ ounces kale, washed and finely chopped

5 scallions, trimmed and thinly sliced

chopped fresh flat-leaf parsley, to serve

Start with the sticky braised beef. Preheat the oven to 300°F.

Add half of the olive oil to an ovenproof Dutch oven over medium heat and sauté the bacon until they have browned and rendered their fat. Remove from the dish.

Season the beef chunks with 1 teaspoon salt. Brown them in small batches in the dish, making sure you get a good brown crust on the meat, as this is the basis of much of the flavor in the braise. If you crowd the pan, the meat will limply stew rather than crisply sear—you don't want this. When the meat is brown all over, remove it from the dish and set it aside. Repeat with the remaining beef and if the dish ever seems too dry, add a little more olive oil.

Once all the meat is done, add the remaining olive oil, then the carrots, onions, mushrooms, and garlic (it's fine if there is some residue from the meat clinging to the bottom). Sauté for 5 to 10 minutes over medium heat to soften the vegetables a little and to add a hint of color.

Return the bacon and meat (and any juices that have leached out) into the dish. Stir to combine, then pour in the stock and Worcestershire sauce. There should be enough liquid to just come to the top of the meat. If it doesn't, add some more stock or water so that the majority of the stew is covered, but some bits pop out the top like floating islands.

Turn the heat up to high and let the stock come to a boil. As soon as it comes to a boil, take the pan off the heat, put the lid on and place in the preheated oven for 2 hours.

After 2 hours, take off the lid and bake for another hour. This will help the sauce to reduce.

When done, the meat should flake apart, the carrots and onions should be pliable and soft, and the sauce sticky and rich. If you're not quite at that point, return the stew to the oven. You could also cook this on low in a slow cooker all day.

To make the white-bean colcannon, use a stick blender or food processor to purée the beans with the milk until very smooth.

Put the kale and any water that's still clinging to the leaves in a saucepan over medium heat. Stir for about 1 to 2 minutes until the kale has begun to soften. Add the bean purée and scallions and stir to heat through and combine, but be careful not to let it catch on the bottom of the pan. If it seems a little dry or begins to catch, add a few tablespoons water or milk. Taste and season with salt and pepper.

Serve the sticky braised beef spooned on top of the white-bean colcannon and top with chopped parsley.

BRAISED CHICKEN WITH WHITE BEANS, MUSTARD, AND CIDER

Serves 4

The original iteration of this dish involved rabbit. It went hunting for all the flavors of Normandy and clamped them together in one pot. Its appeal lay in the perfect balance between the tang of the mustard and the sweetness of the apple cider. Yet I know that any recipe that starts with "joint your rabbit" may cause half of you to turn the page instantly. And so I've altered it for you, but mostly I've done it for my doppelgänger. You see, there's another Tori. We sat next to each other in a slate-gray and Pantone 485 Red office for three years. We were two women in our late twenties, doing exactly the same job, with the same first name in a small team of four. Our birthdays are separated by just a day, we have identical initials, matching freckles on the top of our right ears, and a shared, macabre fascination with sharks. Yet, unlike me, Tori has a pet rabbit called Rudy who is one of the great loves of her life. So out of respect for them both I can now happily confirm that this one-pot, slow-carb wonder works just as well with chicken thighs on the bone as it does with a bunny. Phew.

1 tablespoon olive oil
6 skinless chicken thighs on the bone
2 slices of bacon, cut into thin strips
4 large shallots or 2 onions, peeled and cut into slim half-moons
1 garlic clove, peeled and thinly sliced
4 sprigs of fresh thyme
8 prunes, pitted
1¼ cups apple cider
1 x 14-ounce can of cannellini or lima beans, rinsed
½ tablespoon Dijon mustard
1 tablespoon crème fraîche (optional)
sea salt and freshly ground black pepper

Preheat the oven to 350°F.

Add the olive oil to an ovenproof Dutch oven over medium–high heat and sear the chicken pieces on each side until you have a light golden color. Remove the chicken pieces and set them aside.

In the same dish, fry the bacon for a minute or so until the fat has rendered and it starts to crisp up. Add the shallots or onions, garlic, and a few picked thyme leaves and sauté for 5 to 7 minutes until the shallots or onions have softened.

Add the browned chicken pieces and prunes to the dish. Pour in the cider and turn up the heat. Bring to a boil and use a spoon to scrape up any flavor that's darkened on the bottom of the dish.

Fold in the beans, mustard, and the remaining thyme sprigs. The liquid should come halfway up the chicken pieces, so add a little more water if it doesn't. Clamp the lid on and bake in the preheated oven for 1½ to 2 hours. The chicken should easily pull off the bone and the sauce be sticky and rich.

Serve the chicken over the onion and bean mixture. Add a teaspoon of crème fraîche if you want things a little richer. Season with salt and pepper to taste.

QUINOA-STUFFED MUSHROOMS

Serves 2

Food is a lovely way of bringing people together; of making us feel included, wanted, and respected. Unless it's the festive season and you've committed to serving turkey, bread, and sausage stuffing and later find at your table a vegetarian, a gluten-intolerant, and a couple who are trying to lay off the white carbs. Oops. This is a dish which can help you avoid that scenario. It's a sort of stuffing, but instead of ducking inside a bird, it sits in the bellies of mushrooms. Quinoa stands in for bread and there are two types of cheese for hearty stickability. Nestled in with it all are all sorts of woodsy champions; rosemary, garlic, a garland of wilted spinach, and for a little sweet tang, dried blueberries. They're also lovely made with small white mushrooms as a canapé, or medium mushrooms as a side dish. Add a splodge of crème fraîche just before serving and they're downright civil and welcoming. And if all else goes astray, know they go very well with a glass of fizz.

2 or more large Portobello mushrooms (approximately 9 ounces in total)
2 tablespoons olive oil
2 garlic cloves, peeled and finely diced
2 teaspoons fresh rosemary leaves, finely chopped
¼ cup quinoa, cooked in ½ cup water for 15 minutes until plumped, or scant ⅔ cup cooked quinoa
3¼ ounces baby spinach, roughly chopped
¼ cup grated Parmesan
3 tablespoons/2¼ ounces Boursin cheese (or soft goat cheese)
3 tablespoons dried blueberries
2 tablespoons slivered almonds
2 tablespoons pumpkin seeds
crème fraîche and freshly ground black pepper, to serve

Preheat the oven to 350°F.

Pull the stems out of all the mushrooms, dice them, and set them aside. Place the mushrooms, dark belly side up, on a baking sheet.

Put the olive oil in a skillet over medium heat. Add the garlic and rosemary and sauté gently until they start to soften, then add the diced mushroom stems and sauté until soft.

Add the cooked quinoa and the spinach and stir until the spinach wilts. Fold in the cheeses and the dried blueberries. Stir until the cheeses have melted through the quinoa and spinach. Spoon the mixture into the dark bellies of the mushrooms. Scatter the tops with the almonds and pumpkin seeds.

Bake the mushrooms in the preheated oven for about 25 minutes, or until they are cooked and the almonds are toasted. Serve with a splash of crème fraîche and some black pepper.

TIP: *If you can't find dried blueberries, substitute with dried cranberries or currants. Similarly, if pumpkin seeds prove a stretch, just use more slivered almonds or add some pine nuts. These mushrooms can be prepared ahead of time and left in the refrigerator on a baking sheet covered in plastic wrap. Just remove the plastic wrap and bake when wanted.*

Once upon a time, for me dessert was all about glorious heft. There was nothing more satisfying than the podge of a pudding. Bread and butter, summer berry, sticky toffee, and lemon delicious were my most beloved. It took a lot to stop me from going back for seconds of each of them. These days I've found satisfaction and delight in sweets that take a brighter, lighter tack. Whether it's fresh pit fruits in an almond-based clafoutis, or the spiced warmth of cinnamon-poached pears or a rhubarb crumble with a slow-carb topping, these are the flavors which now bring me the greatest joy. I love these desserts because the majority of them work just as well for me as they do for my gluten-intolerant friends. I love them because most of them are a breeze to make (there need only be three ingredients in the chocolate mousse and the batter for the loaf cakes can be made in a blender in four minutes). And I love them because of how they make me feel. Sure there's some sugar here and the occasional indulgence of chocolate (The Hungry One would hazard that a life without chocolate is not much of a life at all).

I'm not suggesting that the leanest version of you will be eating dessert every night. But when Saturday night or a celebration rolls around, these are the recipes I reach for. And these are the ones which have me scraping my plate for every last taste.

MOREISH
DESSERTS

LATTE CUSTARDS AND CHOCOLATE HAZELNUT CHEWS

Makes 4 custards and 16 to 18 chews

My husband, The Hungry One, is a man with clear tastes and preferences. He likes chocolate. He loves coffee—perhaps a little too much. But curiously, top of all things, he values texture in his food. And when it comes to a cookie, it's the chew which is key. These choc-hazelnut cookies are the ultimate cookie to him: they're intensely flavored with cocoa and pull lightly at your teeth. They're also somewhat magical in their make up—there are no flour, butter, or raising agents to contend with, just egg whites, cocoa, and confectioners' sugar. A few nuts for bite and a little sprinkle of salt will really help them stand out. What they call for on the side is something silken to dunk them into. If you're entertaining, these latte custards can be prepared ahead of time and left to rest in the refrigerator. They're an absolute doddle to make. And best of all, they'll make use of the egg yolks you've got left over from your cookies. Which is a good thing, since one of the only things The Hungry One doesn't like is waste.

Chocolate hazelnut chews
4 egg whites
3 pinches of salt
1 cup unsweetened cocoa
scant 2½ cups confectioners' sugar
1 cup blanched hazelnuts, roughly chopped
  (set aside a few whole hazelnuts to decorate, if you like)

Latte custards
1¼ cups milk
2 shots (60 ml) of espresso or 2 tablespoons strong filter
  coffee (you can use decaf if you prefer)
4 egg yolks
1 whole egg
½ cup superfine sugar
¾ ounce semisweet chocolate, grated

Equipment
baking sheet lined with parchment paper
4 ramekins, 7-ounce capacity, greased

To make the chocolate hazelnut chews, preheat the oven to 350°F.

In a very clean bowl and using an electric whisk on medium speed, whisk the egg whites and a pinch of the salt for 2 minutes, or until the eggs are foaming. Gently rain in the cocoa and confectioners' sugar and beat for another 2 to 3 minutes until you have a glossy, well-incorporated mixture that stands up in peaks. Gently fold in the chopped hazelnuts.

Use a tablespoon to portion and transfer the mixture in mounds onto the lined baking sheet, leaving 1¼ inches between the cookies to allow them to spread while baking. Decorate with whole hazelnuts, if you like. Sprinkle the remaining salt over the tops of the cookies. Bake them in the preheated oven for 20 minutes, or until cracks appear on the tops of cookies and you can peel them off the baking sheet. If they stick to the base, return them to the oven for a few more minutes. Transfer them to a wire rack to cool while you make the latte custards.

Reduce the oven temperature to 325°F and put the prepared ramekins in a roasting dish.

Put the milk and espresso in a small saucepan over low heat and bring to a simmer.

In a bowl, whisk together the egg yolks, whole egg, and sugar until the sugar has dissolved and the mixture is pale. Add one-quarter of a cup of the simmered latte to the bowl and mix well, then gradually add the rest of the latte in a gentle stream. Try not to make it too foamy.

Pour the latte custard into a pitcher through a strainer and try to skim off any foam on the top. Now pour it into the ramekins. Boil some water and transfer the dish or ramekins to the oven, leaving the oven door open. Pour the boiling water into the roasting dish until it comes halfway up the sides of the ramekins.

Bake the custards in the oven for 45 minutes, or until they just wobble in the center when you shuffle them. Chill for 1 hour or so, or until ready to serve. Serve with grated chocolate on top and the chocolate hazelnut chews on the side for dunking.

CLEMENTINE TARTA DE SANTIAGO

Serves 6 to 8

*I first tasted Tarta de Santiago ("cake of St. James")
in the back streets of Madrid, but it was at London's
Borough Market that I really fell for its charms. There
are few finer ways to spend an hour on a Thursday
afternoon than with a flat white from Monmouth
or Elliot's and a sliver of flourless almond cake
from beneath the glass canister on the counter of
the Brindisa store. I'd often find myself still licking
cinnamon and confectioners' sugar from my fingertips
while looking out across the Thames to St. Pauls—and
occasionally pinching myself. Life can sometimes
be very sweet. An authentic Tarta de Santiago is
flavored with orange, though I find the genial twinkle
of clementine works just as well. A pile of poached
clementine segments are just the thing to place in the
center of the cake prior to serving. Meanwhile, the
syrup makes an excellent sticky drizzle (and any left
over is a real treat as a base for a cocktail—try shaking
a dribble of it with gin and Campari over ice).*

5 eggs
generous 1 cup superfine sugar
2¾ cups ground almonds
grated zest of 1 clementine or mandarin
½ teaspoon ground cinnamon

Poached clementines
6 clementines
1¼ cups superfine sugar
2½ cups water

To serve
confectioners' sugar, for dusting
scant ¼ cup roughly chopped almonds
Greek yogurt

Equipment
9-inch springform cake pan, greased and lined with
    parchment paper

To poach the clementines, wash them and then prick
them with a fork at the top, the bottom and 5 times
around the circumference of the fruit.

Take a saucepan large enough to hold the clementines.
Put the sugar and water in the pan over low heat and
stir until the sugar has dissolved. Add the clementines
and simmer, uncovered, for 30 to 45 minutes, rotating
them occasionally until the skins are very soft and
a fork easily slides in. Let the clementines cool
in the syrup until they are cool enough to handle.

Slip the fruit from the skins and remove any obvious
seeds. Place the segments in a bowl and return the
skins to the sugar syrup. Simmer the syrup for another
20 minutes until it has reduced by half. Now you can
either chop the skins into slivers and disperse them
through the syrup, or discard them.

Preheat the oven to 350°F.

Put the eggs and sugar in a bowl and use an electric
whisk to beat them until thick and pale. Fold in the
ground almonds, fresh clementine or mandarin zest,
and cinnamon.

Transfer the batter to the prepared cake pan and bake
in the preheated oven for 40 to 45 minutes or until a
skewer inserted in the middle comes out clean. Set the
pan on a wire rack for 10 minutes before removing the
cake from the pan.

Serve the cake warm and dusted with confectioners'
sugar, with the poached clementine segments, warm
syrup, chopped almonds, and some Greek yogurt.

TIP: *Beyond clementines, you could also tweak the
recipe by using lemon, lime, or orange zest. Or triple
the quantity of cinnamon and add some ground
ginger and allspice for a Christmassy twist.*

YOGURT PANNA COTTAS WITH CINNAMON-POACHED PEARS

Serves 4

These cinnamon-braised pears are as romantic as an afternoon stroll over brittle amber leaves. All they cry out for is a cool and elegant companion. Rather than the heft of cream, the lactic tang of yogurt makes these panna cottas a considerate dessert for everyone, particularly since they're easily made earlier in the day and forgotten about until just before serving. When it comes to the pears, you'll probably find firm-textured fruit will poach better, drinking in the flavored syrup while maintaining their arched shape even after a spell in the pot. For anyone worried about extricating the panna cottas from their molds, here's a trick: if you swipe the inside of your plastic cups with a little neutral oil before pouring the mix in, when set they should easily shirk away from the edge before slinking onto the plate. Alternatively, you could set the panna cottas in small bowls and serve them with the fruit and syrup forming a shallow chestnut pool on top.

Yogurt panna cottas
scant 1 cup pouring cream
¼ cup superfine sugar
2 gold-strength gelatin leaves
scant 1¼ cups Greek yogurt
1 teaspoon neutral-tasting oil

Cinnamon pears
4 cups water
generous 1 cup brown sugar
2 cinnamon sticks
4 Beurré Bosc pears, peeled, cored, and quartered
4 tablespoon walnuts, roughly chopped

Equipment
4 plastic cups or shallow bowls

Begin the panna cottas at least 4 hours before you want to serve them. Put the cream and sugar in a saucepan over low heat and bring it to a simmer, stirring until the sugar has dissolved.

Meanwhile, submerge the gelatin leaves in a bowl of cold water for a few minutes until they become pliable and slippery.

Squeeze the soaked gelatin leaves well and add them to the warm cream. Whisk with a balloon whisk until the gelatin has dissolved. Add the yogurt and whisk gently until smooth.

Swipe the insides of plastic cups with the oil on some paper towels. If you are serving the panna cottas in shallow bowls, there's no need to oil them. Pour the panna cotta mixture into the cups and refrigerate for 4 hours or overnight to set.

To make the cinnamon pears, take a saucepan large enough to hold the pears. Put the water, sugar, and cinnamon sticks in the pan over medium heat. Bring it to a simmer and let the sugar dissolve.

Meanwhile, cut out a circle of parchment paper the same size as the pan, and then cut a small hole out of the middle. This is your cartouche. Add the pears to the pan and cover with the cartouche. Simmer (without the lid) at a gentle blip for 15 to 25 minutes until the point of a knife easily slides into the pears. Pluck the pears from the liquid and boil the syrup over high heat until it has reduced by half.

Just before you are ready to serve, use your index finger to pull the set panna cottas away from the edge of the cup—this will allow air in and break the seal. Place a plate over the mouth of the cup, flip them both over, and let the panna cotta slink down onto the plate. Serve with the pears, a drizzle of syrup, and the walnuts over the top.

TIP: *Please bear in mind that using a cartouche with the center cleaved out for poaching the pears may seem like extra work, but it's worth it: it helps ensure that all of the pears remain submerged in the syrup, giving you more consistent texture across the fruit.*

CHIA, MANGO, COCONUT, AND MACADAMIA TRIFLE

Serves 4

If there's a taste of a Sydney summer, it's probably an errant drip from a ripe mango as it traces from your pinky down to your elbow. Often while chasing it you'll collect the faint taste of coconut-scented sunscreen. If, like me, every now and again you miss that taste so badly it hurts, this dessert may help. Layered in glasses, it uses plump orbs of chia in place of custard or cake. Lychees and macadamias add some more textural interest, but the real hero is the mango. Of course this is best when made with spanking-fresh fruit—but here's a secret. This dessert is also something to keep in your back pocket when you're stuck inside on a gray day with only cans and packages at your disposal. Take a can of sliced mango, a can of coconut milk, and a can of lychees. Drain, blend, mix, and serve. It's just a trifling effort for a terrific dessert. Note: this also works well as part of a brunch or breakfast spread.

scant ½ cup chia seeds
1¾ cups coconut milk
1 x 15-ounce can of mango pieces, drained,
  or 2 medium mangos, peeled and seeded
1 x 15-ounce can of lychees, drained,
  or 20 lychees, shelled and pitted
2 tablespoons macadamias, roughly chopped

Whisk together the chia seeds and coconut milk.

Using a stick blender or food processor, blitz three-quarters of the canned or fresh mango until you have a smooth purée. Slice the remaining mango into slivers and cut the lychees in half and set them aside.

Swirl the mango purée through the chia-coconut mixture and divide half the mixture between 4 glasses.

Add a layer of sliced mango and lychee halves. Top with the mango-chia-coconut mixture and place in the refrigerator for 2 hours or overnight to set. Top with the remaining sliced mango and lychee halves and the macadamias just before serving.

TUTTI FRUTTI CLAFOUTIS

Serves 4

A clafoutis' genus lies somewhere between a pancake and a puffed fruit pudding. A French dessert, it is classically made with cherries still carrying their pits in their bellies. The pits gift an almond twinge to the batter but also mean it can be wise to have a dentist on speed-dial while serving it. While cherries are gorgeous, to me the potential rhyming novelty of serving a tutti frutti clafoutis is way too good to pass up. Reach for as wide a bounty of pit fruits as you dare; pitted nectarines, peaches, apricots, cherries, and plums are all wicked inclusions. Either make it in four petite pans, or serve as slices with vanilla ice cream pooling over the top. While this is an easy dessert to pull together for a small group, it is also lovely for brunch. It's best hot, but there's no reason why you can't eat the leftovers cold the next day with yogurt.

scant 1 cup ground almonds
2 tablespoons cornstarch
4 tablespoons superfine sugar
generous 1 cup whole milk
2 eggs, lightly beaten
2 egg yolks
1¼ pounds mixed pit fruits, e.g. plums, peaches, nectarines,
  apricots, cherries
1½ tablespoons unsalted butter
handful of slivered almonds
ice cream or yogurt, to serve (optional)

Equipment
9-inch non-stick skillet with a heatproof handle,
  or 9-inch round baking dish

Preheat the oven to 400°F.

Whisk the ground almonds, cornstarch, and half the sugar into the milk, beaten eggs, and egg yolks until you have a smooth batter.

Pit and slice the fruit into halves or chunks if they're large peaches or nectarines. Place them in the skillet or baking dish, dot them with dabs of the butter, and scatter the remaining sugar over the top. Bake in the preheated oven for 10 minutes to soften. Remove the pan from the oven and leave the oven on.

Pour the batter over the baked fruit, scatter the slivered almonds over the top, and bake in the oven for 20 minutes, or until the clafoutis has puffed up and the almonds are toasted.

Eat the clafoutis warm, with ice cream—or cold, for breakfast, with yogurt.

PEANUT BUTTER AND JAM PUDDINGS

Makes 12 small puddings, or serves 6 (most people will probably find it hard to eat just one)

For the longest time, I never understood the appeal of combining peanut butter with jelly or jam. It was the stickiness of it all that upset me. That was until I twigged that combining a touch of salt with the sweet is one of the great secrets of the universe. It pulls everything into balance—and it's exactly what's at work here. If you like, an extra sprinkling of salt on the top of these deceptively light puddings manages to amplify the sweetness of the berries hiding inside. Serve them with a dollop of jam and some roasted peanuts on the top for crunch. And perhaps a little cream or ice cream on the side.

4 eggs
1 cup chunky peanut butter
½ cup + 2 tablespoons superfine sugar
1 teaspoon sea salt flakes
¼ cup vegetable oil
½ teaspoon baking soda
½ teaspoon baking powder
½ cup milk
generous ½ cup fresh or frozen raspberries

To serve
¼ cup raspberry jam, warmed with a small splash of water
2 tablespoons roasted peanuts
vanilla ice cream

Equipment
12-cup muffin pan, greased and dusted with flour

Preheat the oven to 350°F.

In a bowl, whisk together all the ingredients, except the raspberries, until they are well combined and smooth. Divide the mixture between the cups of the muffin pan.

Divide the raspberries between the puddings, gently prodding them into their middles.

Bake the puddings in the preheated oven for about 20 minutes, or until they are golden and puffed and a skewer inserted in the middle comes out clean (but for a bit of raspberry smear).

Let cool in the muffin pan for 5 minutes, then carefully remove each pudding. Serve with a drizzling of the jam-syrup, the peanuts, and some vanilla ice cream.

SALZBURGER NOCKERL, OR BERRIES AND CLOUDS

Serves 4

There are only 150,000 people who live in Salzburg. Yet every year more than 300,000 Sound of Music devotees will make a pilgrimage to the city. Sure they might be interested in seeing Mozart's birthplace. Others might want to dine at arguably the oldest restaurant in Europe (circa 803), drink at the Stiegl brewery and wander by a blue river on a clear day. But really, most have come to enjoy tea with jam and bread, crisp apple strudel, and schnitzel with noodles. Once you've sung do-re-mi enough and clamored out of your carb hole, if you haven't gone into complete sugar shock (from the food and the movie), there's always the option of Salzburger Nockerl for dessert. This local specialty involves berries (traditionally raspberries, but in deference to the von Trapps' berry-picking escapades I've opted for blueberries) topped with buoyant clouds of souffléed meringue. The meringues are classically formed into three peaks to resemble the hills bordering the city. It's a dessert best served warm with some custard on the side. And afterward, there's no need for you to climb every mountain, but a hike up at least one small hill will help slake some of the indulgence.

3 cups blueberries (defrosted and drained if frozen)
grated zest and juice of ½ lemon
scant ½ cup confectioners' sugar, plus extra for dusting
7 eggs, separated
a pinch of salt
generous ⅓ cup superfine sugar
1½ tablespoons cornstarch
custard, to serve (optional)

Equipment
8-inch square baking dish, greased

Preheat the oven to 350°F.

Put the berries, lemon zest, and juice in the prepared baking dish and sprinkle with the confectioners' sugar.

If you have an electric whisk, now is the time to use it. Put the egg whites and salt in a very clean bowl and whisk until the eggs are foamy. Add ¼ cup of the superfine sugar, a tablespoon at a time, and whisk well between each addition. Keep whisking until the whites have quadrupled in size and are stiff enough to hold their shape when you hold the bowl upside down (over your head, if you're brave enough).

Put the egg yolks and the remaining sugar in a separate bowl and whisk until the eggs are fluffy. Beat in the cornstarch until incorporated. Finally, carefully fold the mixture into the beaten egg whites with a metal spoon, in 3 stages, trying to maintain as much air in the mixture as possible.

Portion the mixture over the berries in 3 mounds to resemble the 3 mountains that surround Salzburg.

Bake the pudding in the preheated oven for 30 minutes, or until a light crust has formed on the outside and the interior of the egg topping is no longer liquidy—a skewer inserted in the middle of the topping should come out clean. Turn the oven off and leave the pudding inside with the door closed for an additional 15 minutes before removing it and serving it immediately. Dust with confectioners' sugar and serve with a little custard, if you like.

PASSIONFRUIT AND RASPBERRY NOUGAT PARFAIT

Serves 8

This parfait carries me straight to an Australian Christmas, when the air is muggy and your hair is still soggy from the last dip in the swimming pool. My mother would always make a version of this, studded with berries and decked with toasted nuts to be sliced as the last taste in our Christmas Eve holiday meal. To this day, the original recipe remains scrawled on three scraps of paper and spends 50 weeks of the year lying in a drawer in her house, along with gold wrapping paper and spools of red ribbon. My take is a little sunnier, rippling the sparkle of passionfruit curd through the cooled ricotta and whipped cream. While you could weave all of the curd through the dessert, I like to keep some of it aside, either to drape over the top of the pudding, or to swirl through yogurt the next day. Christmas breakfast has rarely tasted so good.

Passionfruit curd
4 egg yolks
½ cup + 2 tablespoons superfine sugar
scant ½ cup lemon juice
grated zest of 1 lemon
pulp scooped out of 2 passionfruit
¼ cup unsalted butter

Parfait
1¾ cups ricotta
scant 1 cup superfine sugar
1¼ cups whipping cream
3½ ounces nougat, chopped
scant 1 cup fresh or frozen raspberries
¾ cup cooled Passionfruit Curd (see below)

Equipment
8 x 5-inch loaf pan, bottom and sides double-lined with
  parchment paper

For the passionfruit curd, whisk together the egg yolks and sugar until they are fluffy. Transfer to a saucepan with the remaining ingredients and set over medium–low heat. Stir until the mixture thickens like mayonnaise. If it is lumpy, strain it before pouring it into jars to cool.

For the parfait, blend the ricotta and sugar until smooth. In a separate bowl, whisk the cream until soft peaks form. Fold all the ingredients together, then swirl through them three-quarters of a cup of the passionfruit curd until you have a ripple effect.

Spoon the mixture into the prepared loaf pan and freeze it for 6 to 8 hours. To serve, turn the parfait out of the pan, slice it, and arrange the slices on a platter. Put the slices in the refrigerator for 30 minutes before serving to allow them to soften to the right consistency. Dollop any remaining passionfruit curd over the top of the slices.

TIP: *This must be made at least 6 hours before serving. It benefits from softening in the refrigerator for 15 to 20 minutes before cutting.*

BAKED RICOTTA-STUFFED PEACHES

Serves 2 as a modest, light dessert (but if you want a more robust serving, scale up as needed)

There are dishes in a repertoire that are inspired by a place, igniting memories of wonderful times away. And then there are others which act more as Post-it notes; an edible reminder to yourself that one day, you will make it there. For me, the place is the Amalfi coast, and the dish is this. Every time I roast sweet peaches, plumping their bellies with nutmeg-spiced ricotta first, I imagine myself strolling the steep streets of Positano. I may be eating this in my pyjamas at home, but after two bites of this I'm gone.

1 large (or 2 medium) peach, halved and pitted
3 tablespoons ricotta
1 tablespoon brown sugar
½ teaspoon ground cinnamon
½ teaspoon grated nutmeg
1 tablespoon chopped pistachios
honey and Greek yogurt or crème fraîche, to serve (optional)

Preheat the oven to 350°F.

Use a melon baller to hollow out the peach a little further, where the pit was. Place the peach halves, cut side up, in individual ramekins or snuggled up to one another in a baking dish.

Mix together the ricotta, sugar, and spices. Transfer the mix into the bellies of the peaches. Bake the peaches in the preheated oven for 15 to 20 minutes until the ricotta has bronzed and the peaches have softened.

Serve the peaches either warm or at room temperature, topped with the pistachios and drizzled with honey. Some Greek yogurt or crème fraîche on the side would also be a nice addition.

CHOCOLATE, BLACK BEAN, AND CHERRY CAKE

Makes 8 to 10 slices

I've become a little evangelical about these cakes. Why? For one, they're the simplest cakes I've ever encountered. You have a blender or a food processor? You have a loaf pan? You have an oven? Done. There's no flour, so they're perfect for your gluten-intolerant friends. And together they form two sides of one joyous coin. The first is dark with chocolate and will satisfy even the most insane hormonal craving. The second is angelic with rose water, almonds, and raspberries. These are both my go-to, emergency cakes, taking turns week on week. They're smart enough to be served warm with crème fraîche or heavy cream. They're sturdy enough for lunch boxes. They're not so evil that you couldn't justify a slice at 3 p.m. with a cup of tea after you've tottered to the post office. I don't want to get too crazy here, but there's every chance that these cakes may change your life.

1 x 14-ounce can of black beans, rinsed
3 eggs
½ cup superfine sugar
1 shot (1 ounce) of espresso or 1 tablespoon strong filter coffee (you can use decaf if you prefer)
3 tablespoons unsweetened cocoa
1 teaspoon baking powder (check it is gluten-free if cooking for a celiac crowd)
scant 1 cup cherries, pitted (can be frozen, and you can also substitute other berries), plus extra to serve
confectioners' sugar, yogurt, crème fraîche, or fresh cherries, to serve (optional)

Equipment
8 x 5-inch loaf pan, greased and lined with parchment paper

Preheat the oven to 350°F.

Using a stick blender and mixing bowl, blender or food processor, combine all the ingredients except the cherries and blitz until smooth. The batter will appear quite liquidy but don't worry. Pour the batter into the prepared loaf pan and scatter the cherries over the top.

Bake the loaf in the preheated oven for 35 minutes, or until a skewer inserted in the middle comes out with a few fudgy crumbs on it.

Let cool in the pan for 5 minutes, then turn it out. Dust with confectioners' sugar and serve warm with more cherries, yogurt, or crème fraîche for dessert, or let it cool and enjoy it with a cup of tea or coffee.

RASPBERRY, WHITE BEAN, AND ROSE CAKE

Makes 8 to 10 slices

1 x 14-ounce can of cannellini beans, rinsed
3 eggs
½ cup superfine sugar
1 tablespoon rose water
3 tablespoons ground almonds
1 teaspoon baking powder (check it is gluten-free if cooking for a celiac crowd)
1 cup raspberries (can be frozen, and you can also substitute other berries, or pitted cherries), plus extra to serve
confectioners' sugar, yogurt, or crème fraîche, to serve (optional)

Equipment
8 x 5-inch loaf pan, greased and lined with parchment paper

Preheat the oven to 350°F.

Using a stick blender and mixing bowl, blender, or food processor, combine all the ingredients except the raspberries and blitz until smooth. The batter will appear quite liquidy but don't worry. Pour the batter into the prepared loaf pan and scatter the raspberries over the top.

Bake the loaf in the preheated oven for 35 minutes, or until a skewer inserted in the middle comes out with a few fudgy crumbs on it.

Let cool in the pan for 5 minutes, then turn it out. Dust with confectioners' sugar and serve warm with more raspberries, yogurt, or crème fraîche for dessert, or let it cool and enjoy it with a cup of tea or coffee.

RHUBARB, APPLE, AND BERRY SLOW CRUMBLE

Serves 4

The boundaries between a crumble, a crisp, a buckle, and a slump are blurry. All seem to involve poached or baked fruit and a topping usually melding sugar, butter, and a grain. When it comes to my dessert I'm less interested in definitional purity and more intrigued by having something that tastes terrific. The golden thing about this crumble isn't just the way that the tartness of the rhubarb is mellowed by segments of apple and oozing berries. Nor is it the wink of spice in the cinnamon or ginger, or the crunch from the slivered almonds and toasted oats. It's the other bits that make you feel good: the ground flaxseed and the sneaky smashed banana. An overripe banana mushed into the topping helps pull down the quantity of raw sugar and contributes both a delicious caramel–sweetness and a rustic chew to the topping. This may be categorized as a "slow crumble," but in our house, it never lasts long. Once again, while this is a delicious dessert, it's also worth considering as a celebratory brunch or breakfast option, with Greek yogurt instead of ice cream.

scant ½ cup unsalted butter, chilled and cubed,
  plus 2 tablespoons for the fruit
1 cup rolled oats
generous ⅓ cup ground flaxseed
scant 1 cup slivered almonds
2 tablespoons brown sugar
1 ripe banana, mashed
2 teaspoons ground ginger
2 teaspoons ground cinnamon
5 sticks (9 ounces) of rhubarb, cut into 1½-inch sticks
4 Pink Lady apples, peeled, cored, and cut into eighths
scant 1 cup blackberries
Greek yogurt, crème fraîche, heavy cream, or ice cream,
  to serve

Equipment
large, shallow baking dish, greased

Preheat the oven 350°F.

To make a crumble topping, put the scant ½ cup butter, oats, flaxseed, almonds, sugar, banana, ginger, and cinnamon in a bowl. Use your fingers to mash everything together into a rustic tumble. It should be rough and lumpy. Refrigerate the topping until ready to bake.

Put the rhubarb and apple and half the blackberries in a saucepan with the 2 tablespoons butter and cook over medium heat for 10 to 15 minutes until the rhubarb and apple have begun to soften.

Transfer the softened fruit to the prepared baking dish and dot with the remaining berries.

Scatter the crumble topping over the fruit, ensuring there are lots of craggy edges.

Bake the crumble in the preheated oven for 30 minutes, or until the top is bronzed and crisp. Serve hot with Greek yogurt, crème fraîche, heavy cream, or ice cream. Or enjoy cold, for breakfast.

PEPPERMINT CHOCOLATE MOUSSE WITH PISTACHIOS

Serves 2, but can easily be scaled up as needed

It's hard not to love a three-ingredient mousse. All that's required is a hot cup of tea, a few chunks of dark chocolate, and some egg whites. This recipe had a Goldilocks start in life. Two egg whites were too flat. Four muffled the taste of the chocolate. But three were just right. While this version uses peppermint tea, recalling the retro tastes of my parents' mint "After Eight" chocolates which were reserved for occasional dinner parties, you could easily recruit other flavors. Earl or Lady Grey tea would contribute some pleasing aromas, ginger tea would be a refreshing change or a long black coffee would give it a little extra get-up-and-go. Experiment to your heart's content. Something to bear in mind: this is a mousse that is even better the next day, making it the perfect thing to quickly prepare on a Thursday night if you have people coming over after work on a Friday.

1 peppermint tea bag
scant ½ cup boiling water
14 ounces semisweet chocolate, chopped
3 egg whites
a pinch of salt
8 fresh mint leaves
2 teaspoons pistachios, toasted and chopped

Equipment
2 x 7-ounce ramekins

Steep the peppermint tea bag in the boiling water until the water is cool enough for you to hold your finger in it for 5 seconds. Remove the tea bag and discard it.

Put 3½ ounces of the chocolate and the peppermint tea in a small saucepan over low heat. Stir until two-thirds of the chocolate has melted, then take the pan off the heat.

Add the remaining chocolate to the pan and stir it, off the heat, until it has melted. This will help temper the chocolate a little, making it glossier and preventing it from becoming grainy.

Transfer the melted mint chocolate to a bowl and stir until it is smooth and has come to room temperature. Add the egg whites and salt and beat with an electric whisk for 4 to 6 minutes until ribbons form in the mixture.

Pour into the ramekins and refrigerate for 4 to 6 hours or overnight.

Serve the mousses topped with the mint leaves and chopped pistachios.

ORANGE, CHOCOLATE, AND HAZELNUT PUDDINGS

Serves 4

If there are three desserts which sum up the 90s to me it would be tiramisù, sticky date pudding, and soft-centered chocolate puddings. Granted, there were lots of things about that decade which might best be forgotten (combat boots, wallet chains, and platform sandals included), but an oozing fondant isn't one of them. This example uses ground hazelnuts for flour, which also contributes a slight Nutella flavor, while the orange zest contributes a bit of a twist. If you fancy a pronounced "jaffa" flavor in your dessert feel free to use the zest of a whole orange rather than half. These are a great dessert for entertaining, as you can easily prepare the batter in the afternoon and bake to order while the main course is being served; but don't delay in getting them to the table, as the residual heat in the desserts will keep cooking them all the way through. There may be lots of things which have gone out of style, but the molten center of a chocolate pudding is one taste which will never date.

½ cup superfine sugar, plus 1 tablespoon for dusting
¼ cup unsalted butter
1 shot (1 ounce) of espresso
3½ ounces semisweet chocolate (minimum 70% cocoa solids), chopped
2 eggs
grated zest of 1 orange
generous 1 cup ground hazelnuts

To serve
ice cream, Greek yogurt, or crème fraîche

Equipment
4 x 7-ounce ramekins, greased

Preheat the oven to 425°F.

Sprinkle the 1 tablespoon superfine sugar inside a greased ramekin, rolling it around to ensure the sides are evenly covered, then pour the excess sugar into the next ramekin and repeat until they have all been dusted.

Put the butter, espresso, and chocolate in a saucepan over medium heat and stir until melted and smooth. Alternatively, use a microwave.

Put the eggs and ½ cup sugar in a bowl and beat with an electric whisk for 2 to 3 minutes until pale and fluffy. Pour the mixture into the melted chocolate, stir, then fold in half the orange zest and all the ground hazelnuts.

Divide the mixture between the prepared ramekins (about 4 tablespoons each). Put the ramekins on a baking sheet and bake the puddings in the preheated oven for 15 minutes, or until firm to the touch and still slightly molten in the center.

Serve the puddings hot with the remaining orange zest, ice cream, Greek yogurt, or crème fraîche pooling on the crest of each one. If you really wanted to push the boat out, you could swirl some good-quality marmalade with softened vanilla ice cream and refreeze it, then and add a scoop of that on the side (or use some of the syrup from the poached clementines on page 150).

INDEX

A

adzuki beans 10, 11
  miso eggplant with ginger tofu
    and adzuki beans 139
aïoli, red-eye 42
ajo blanco with red grapes 60
ajvar, lentil "meatballs" with tomato
  and 133
all the nanas' chicken, lemon, egg, and
  white bean soup 48
almonds: ajo blanco with red grapes 60
  almond blueberry pancakes 14
  clementine tarta de Santiago 150
  five-spice soy roasted almonds 36
apple cider vinegar 10
apples: green soup 62
  rhubarb, apple, and berry slow
    crumble 167
  savory baked apples with goat curd
    and prosciutto 70
  sort-of-Waldorf salad 101
apricots: chia and apricot quinoa
  porridge 23
artichokes: artichokes with red-eye
  aïoli 42
  cannellini bean, Parmesan, and
    artichoke dip 34
arugula, lemon, and walnut pesto 53
asparagus dippers, gooey eggs with 16
pomegranate molasses 79
avocados: guacamole 26
  shrimp, avocado, and edamame salad
    106

B

bacon: pigs in kimchee blankets 39
  shrimp and quinoa grits 136
  smoked paprika chia frittatas 19
  soft eggs with smoky baked beans 25
bananas: rhubarb, apple, and berry
  slow crumble 167
basil pesto 75
beans 10–11
beef: baked white-bean gnocchi with
  meatballs 122
  pork, beef, and mushroom-stuffed
    cabbage rolls 130
  sticky braised beef 142
beet: duck breasts with roast beet,
  radish, and cocoa 140
  roast beet and carrots with ras el

hanout, mint, and labneh 80
berries and clouds 158
Bircher muesli, chia 22
black beans 10, 11
  black bean, chorizo, sweet potato, and
    coconut bowl 82
  chocolate, black bean, and cherry
    cake 164
  griddled chili peppers stuffed with
    feta, black beans, and pumpkin
    seeds 104
  Mexican baked eggs 26
  piri piri chicken with black beans and
    tomatoes 116
Black Forest slow granola parfaits 30
blackberries: rhubarb, apple, and berry
  slow crumble 167
Bloody Mary tomato soup 54
blue cheese soufflés 120
blueberries: almond blueberry pancakes
  14
  Salzburger nockerl 158
borlotti beans 10, 11
  borlotti beans with roasted pear,
    walnuts, and blue cheese 87
  soft eggs with smoky baked beans 25
  "three beans" with basil pesto 75
Brazil nuts, broccoli steaks with
  chimichurri and 68
broccoli: broccoli steaks with
  chimichurri and Brazil nuts 68
  cauliflower and broccoli gratin 73
  green soup 62
brown rice tea salt, edamame with 38
Brussels sprouts with hazelnuts, lentils,
  and mustard dressing 72
burgers, Moroccan lamb and chickpea
  111
burned butter 80

C

cabbage rolls, pork, beef, and
  mushroom-stuffed 130
cakes: chocolate, black bean, and cherry
  cake 164
  raspberry, white bean, and rose cake
    164
cannellini beans 10, 11
  ajo blanco with red grapes 60
  braised chicken with white beans,
    mustard and cider 144

cannellini bean, Parmesan, and
  artichoke dip 34
  Mediterranean squid stuffed with
    white bean purée and olives 112
  raspberry, white bean, and rose cake
    164
  ribollita 53
  sausages with leeks, caramelized
    onions, mushrooms, and beans
    138
  "three beans" with basil pesto 75
  white sauce 127
carrots: carrot purée 67
  roast beet and carrots with
    ras el hanout, mint, and labneh 80
cauliflower: cauliflower and broccoli
  gratin 73
  cauliflower "couscous" 76
  cauliflower purée 66
chana dal 11
  dal 78
cheese: eggplant "parm" 127
  baked white-bean gnocchi with
    meatballs, mozzarella, and tomato
    122
  blue cheese soufflés 120
  borlotti beans with roasted pear,
    walnuts, and blue cheese 87
  cauliflower and broccoli gratin 73
  feta, mint, lentil, and pistachio
    omelets 20
  griddled chili peppers stuffed with
    feta, black beans, and pumpkin
    seeds 104
  mushroom and goat curd "toasties"
    16
  roasted and fresh tomato skewers
    with mint and halloumi 40
  savory baked apples with goat curd
    and prosciutto 70
  socca with smoked salmon and
    whipped curds 28
  see also ricotta
cherries: Black Forest slow granola
  parfaits 30
  chocolate, black bean, and cherry
    cake 164
chia seeds 9
  chia and apricot quinoa porridge 23
  chia Bircher muesli 22

chia, mango, coconut, and macadamia trifle 155
   peppers stuffed with chia, hummus, and pine nuts 98
   smoked paprika chia frittatas 19
chicken: all the nanas' chicken, lemon, egg, and white bean soup 48
   braised chicken with white beans, mustard, and cider 144
   chicken san choi bow 96
   piri piri chicken with black beans and tomatoes 116
   quinoa aguadito (Peruvian chicken and cilantro soup) 58
   sort-of-Waldorf salad 101
   thyme-roasted chicken legs 134
chickpea flour/gram/besan 10
   socca with smoked salmon and whipped curds 28
chickpeas 10
   chickpeas, leek, apple, and pear salad 75
   chilled curried chickpea soup 57
   kale caesar 84
   lamb shank and fig tagine 128
   Moroccan lamb and chickpea burgers 111
   spiced chickpea bombs 44
chili peppers: griddled chili peppers stuffed with feta, black beans, and pumpkin seeds 104
   Mexican baked eggs 26
   piri piri marinade 116
   yellow split peas with burned butter and orange 80
chimichurri, broccoli steaks with Brazil nuts and 68
chocolate: chocolate, black bean, and cherry cake 164
   chocolate hazelnut chews 148
   duck breasts with roast beet, radish, and cocoa 140
   orange, chocolate, and hazelnut puddings 170
   peppermint chocolate mousse with pistachios 168
chorizo: black bean, chorizo, sweet potato, and coconut bowl 82
   green soup with chorizo almond crumbs 62
choucroute 124
cilantro: quinoa aguadito (Peruvian chicken and cilantro soup) 58
cinnamon coffee protein shake 14
cinnamon-poached pears 152
clafoutis, tutti frutti 155

clementine tarta de Santiago 150
coconut milk: chia, mango, coconut, and macadamia trifle 155
coffee: chocolate, black bean, and cherry cake 164
   cinnamon coffee protein shakes 14
   latte custards 148
colcannon, white-bean 142
cookies: chocolate hazelnut chews 148
cream: passionfruit and raspberry nougat parfait 161
   yogurt panna cottas 152
crudités 34
crumble: rhubarb, apple, and berry slow crumble 167
cucumber: chilled white bean, cucumber, mint, and yogurt soup 56
   raita 108
curried chickpea soup 57
custards, latte 148

D
dal 78
dip, cannellini bean, Parmesan, and artichoke 34
duck breasts with roast beet, radish, and cocoa 140

E
edamame beans: edamame with brown rice tea salt 38
   shrimp, avocado, and edamame salad 106
eggs: feta, mint, lentil, and pistachio omelets 20
   gooey eggs with asparagus dippers 16
   Mexican baked eggs 26
   smoked paprika chia frittatas 19
   soft eggs with smoky baked beans 25
eggplants: eggplant "parm" 127
   miso eggplant with ginger tofu and adzuki beans 139
   smoky eggplant with tomatoes, pickled onion, parsley, and

F
fava bean, fennel, mint, lemon, and Parmesan salad 100
fennel: fava bean, fennel, mint, lemon, and Parmesan salad 100
   fennel purée 66
   sort-of-Waldorf salad 101
feta, mint, lentil, and pistachio omelets 20
figs: lamb shank and fig tagine 128

fishcakes, tuna Niçoise 103
five-spice soy roasted almonds 36
frittatas, smoked paprika chia 19
fritters: quinoa and zucchini fritters 40
   zucchini frites 44
fruit: tutti frutti clafoutis 155

G
gado gado Indonesian vegetable salad 87
garlic: red-eye aïoli 42
gas factor, beans 11
gnocchi, baked white-bean 122
goat curd: mushroom and goat curd "toasties" 16
   savory baked apples with goat curd and prosciutto 70
granola parfaits, Black Forest 30
grapes: ajo blanco with red grapes 60
gratin, cauliflower and broccoli 73
green beans: green bean and tomato salad 92
   "three beans" with basil pesto 75
green soup 62
guacamole 26

H
ham: choucroute 124
   savory baked apples with goat curd and prosciutto 70
   ultimate ham and lentil soup 50
hazelnuts: Brussels sprouts with hazelnuts, lentils, and mustard dressing 72
   chocolate hazelnut chews 148
   orange, chocolate, and hazelnut puddings 170
hummus: peppers stuffed with chia, hummus, and pine nuts 98

I
Indonesian vegetable salad 87

J
jam: peanut butter and jam puddings 156
jamón: jamón salt 38
   ultimate ham and lentil soup 50
jicama/yam beans: chicken san choi bow 96

K
kale: green soup 62
   kale caesar 84
   kale chips with lemon 36
   white-bean colcannon 142

kelp/kombu 11
kidney beans 11
kimchee blankets, pigs in 39

L

lamb: lamb shank and fig tagine 128
    Moroccan lamb and chickpea burgers
    111
latte custards 148
leeks: chickpeas, leek, apple, and pear
    salad 75
lentils 10, 11
    Brussels sprouts with hazelnuts,
    lentils, and mustard dressing 72
    dirty quinoa 114
    feta, mint, lentil, and pistachio
    omelets 20
    green soup 62
    lentil "meatballs" 133
    tandoori salmon with spiced lentils
    and raita 108
    Turkish red lentil soup 51
    ultimate ham and lentil soup 50
lettuce: Moroccan lamb and chickpea
    burgers in lettuce leaves 111
    thyme-roasted chicken legs with
    braised baby lettuce and peas 134
lima beans: baked white-bean gnocchi
    122
    soft eggs with smoky baked beans 25
lychees: chia, mango, coconut, and
    macadamia trifle 155

M

mangos: chia, mango, coconut, and
    macadamia trifle 155
meatballs: baked white-bean gnocchi
    with meatballs 122
    lentil "meatballs" with ajvar and
    tomato 133
Mediterranean squid 112
meringue: Salzburger nockerl 158
Mexican baked eggs 26
milk: cinnamon coffee protein shakes
    14
mint: mint-yogurt dressing 111
    raita 108
miso eggplant 139
Moroccan lamb and chickpea burgers
    111
mousse, peppermint chocolate with
    pistachios 168
muesli, chia Bircher 22
mung beans 11
mushrooms: mushroom and goat curd

"toasties" 16
    pork, beef, and mushroom-stuffed
    cabbage rolls 130
    quinoa-stuffed mushrooms 145
    sausages with leeks, caramelized
    onions, mushrooms, and beans 138
    sticky braised beef 142

N

nougat: passionfruit and raspberry
    nougat parfait 161
nuts: Black Forest slow granola parfaits
    30

O

oats: Black Forest slow granola parfaits
    30
    chia Bircher muesli 22
omelets: feta, mint, lentil, and pistachio
    omelets 20
onions: sausages with leeks,
    caramelized onions, mushrooms,
    and beans 138
    smoky eggplant with tomatoes,
    pickled onion, parsley, and
    pomegranate molasses 79
orange, chocolate, and hazelnut
    puddings 170

P

padrón peppers with jamón salt 38
pancakes: almond blueberry pancakes
    14
    socca with smoked salmon and
    whipped curds 28
panna cottas, yogurt 152
papaya: Thai green papaya salad with
    trout 95
parfait, passionfruit and raspberry
    nougat 161
passionfruit and raspberry nougat
    parfait 161
peaches: baked ricotta-stuffed peaches
    162
    peach pulled pork with dirty quinoa
    114
peanut butter: peanut butter and jam
    puddings 156
    spicy peanut sauce 87
pears: borlotti beans with roasted pear,
    walnuts, and blue cheese 87
    cinnamon-poached pears 152
peas: green soup 62
    pea purée 67
    thyme-roasted chicken legs with
    braised baby lettuce and peas 134

see also split peas
peppermint chocolate mousse 168
peppers: Mexican baked eggs 26
    padrón peppers with jamón salt 38
    peppers stuffed with chia, hummus,
    and pine nuts 98
    piri piri chicken 116
Peruvian chicken and cilantro soup 58
pesto: arugula, lemon, and walnut
    pesto 53
    "three beans" with basil pesto 75
pigs in kimchee blankets 39
pine nuts, peppers stuffed with chia,
    hummus, and 98
pinto beans 11
piri piri chicken 116
pistachio nuts: feta, mint, lentil, and
    pistachio omelets 20
    peppermint chocolate mousse with
    pistachios 168
pork: peach pulled pork with dirty
    quinoa 114
    pork, beef, and mushroom-stuffed
    cabbage rolls 130
porridge, chia and apricot quinoa 23
prosciutto: gooey eggs with asparagus
    dippers 16
    savory baked apples with goat curd
    and prosciutto 70
protein shake, cinnamon coffee 14
purées 66–7

Q

quinoa 9
    chia and apricot quinoa porridge 23
    peach pulled pork with dirty quinoa
    114
    pork, beef, and mushroom-stuffed
    cabbage rolls 130
    quinoa aguadito (Peruvian chicken
    and cilantro soup) 58
    quinoa and zucchini fritters 40
    quinoa-stuffed mushrooms 145
    shrimp and quinoa grits 136

R

radishes: duck breasts with roast beet,
    radish, and cocoa 140
    radishes with butter and truffle salt
    34
raita 108
raspberries: passionfruit and raspberry
    nougat parfait 161
    peanut butter and jam puddings 156
    raspberry, white bean, and rose cake

164

rhubarb, apple, and berry slow crumble 167

ribollita 53

rice malt syrup 10

ricotta: baked ricotta-stuffed peaches 162

   passionfruit and raspberry nougat parfait 161

S

salads: fava bean, fennel, mint, lemon, and Parmesan salad 100

   gado gado Indonesian vegetable salad 87

   green bean and tomato salad 92

   kale caesar 84

   shrimp, avocado, and edamame salad 106

   sort-of-Waldorf salad 101

   Thai green papaya salad with trout 95

salmon: tandoori salmon with spiced lentils and raita 108

salt, jamón 38

Salzburger nockerl 158

san choi bow, chicken 96

sauerkraut: choucroute 124

sausages: choucroute 124

   pigs in kimchee blankets 39

   sausages with leeks, caramelized onions, mushrooms, and beans 138

   soft eggs with smoky baked beans 25

sea bass swaddled in zucchini ribbons 90

seaweed 11

shrimp: shrimp and quinoa grits 136

   shrimp, avocado, and edamame salad 106

smoked paprika chia frittatas 19

smoked salmon: socca with smoked salmon and whipped curds 28

socca with smoked salmon and whipped curds 28

sort-of-Waldorf salad 101

soufflés, blue cheese 120

soups: ajo blanco with red grapes 60

   all the nanas' chicken, lemon, egg, and white bean soup 48

   chilled curried chickpea soup 57

   chilled white bean, cucumber, mint, and yogurt soup 56

   green soup 62

   quinoa aguadito (Peruvian chicken and cilantro soup) 58

   ribollita 53

roast Bloody Mary tomato soup 54

   Turkish red lentil soup 51

   ultimate ham and lentil soup 50

spices 11

split peas 11

   split pea purée 67

   yellow split peas with burned butter and orange 80

squid: Mediterranean squid stuffed with white bean purée and olives 112

sweet potatoes: black bean, chorizo, sweet potato, and coconut bowl 82

T

tagine, lamb shank and fig 128

tandoori salmon 108

tarka seasoning 78

tarta de Santiago, clementine 150

Thai green papaya salad with trout 95

"three beans" with basil pesto 75

thyme-roasted chicken legs 134

tofu: miso eggplant with ginger tofu and adzuki beans 139

tomatoes: baked white-bean gnocchi with meatballs, mozzarella, and tomato 122

   chilled curried chickpea soup 57

   eggplant "parm" 127

   green bean and tomato salad 92

   lentil "meatballs" with ajvar and tomato 133

   Mediterranean squid 112

   Mexican baked eggs 26

   Moroccan lamb and chickpea burgers 111

   piri piri chicken with black beans and tomatoes 116

   pork, beef, and mushroom-stuffed cabbage rolls 130

   roast Bloody Mary tomato soup 54

   roasted and fresh tomato skewers with mint and halloumi 40

   smoked paprika chia frittatas 19

   soft eggs with smoky baked beans 25

trifle: chia, mango, coconut, and macadamia trifle 155

trout, Thai green papaya salad with 95

tuna: tuna Niçoise fishcakes 103

   vitello tonnato 92

Turkish red lentil soup 51

tutti frutti clafoutis 155

V

veal: vitello tonnato 92

vegetables: crudités 34

ribollita 53

   see also peppers, tomatoes *etc*

vinegar, apple cider 10

vitello tonnato 92

W

walnuts: arugula, lemon, and walnut pesto 53

   borlotti beans with roasted pear, walnuts, and blue cheese 87

white beans: ajo blanco with red grapes 60

   all the nanas' chicken, lemon, egg, and white bean soup 48

   baked white-bean gnocchi 122

   braised chicken with white beans, mustard, and cider 144

   cannellini bean, Parmesan, and artichoke dip 34

   chilled white bean, cucumber, mint, and yogurt soup 56

   Mediterranean squid stuffed with white bean purée and olives 112

   raspberry, white bean, and rose cake 164

   ribollita 53

   roast Bloody Mary tomato soup 54

   sausages with leeks, caramelized onions, mushrooms, and beans 138

   soft eggs with smoky baked beans 25

   "three beans" with basil pesto 75

   tuna Niçoise fishcakes 103

   white-bean colcannon 142

   white bean purée 67

white sauce 127

Y

yellow split peas with burned butter and orange 80

yogurt: chia Bircher muesli 22

   chilled white bean, cucumber, mint, and yogurt soup 56

   mint-yogurt dressing 111

   raita 108

   yogurt panna cottas 152

Z

zucchini: zucchini frites 44

   quinoa and zucchini fritters 40

   sea bass swaddled in zucchini ribbons 90

Acknowledgments

Thank you to all the luminous people who helped to make this book possible. It was a degree of serendipity which joined me once again with the remarkable Céline Hughes, without whose eagle eye, I'd be lost. To the rest of the kind folk at Quadrille, in particular Anne Furniss, Arielle Gamble, and Helen Lewis, thank you for your stunning work. And thank you to Clare Hulton for your stewardship in finding this book such a happy home.

Eternal gratitude to Chris Chen for hosting a photoshoot that managed to be elegant, efficient, and welcoming to the whims of an 11-week-old baby boy, and to Kirsty and Nick for making it all come together so smoothly.

Editorial director Anne Furniss
Creative director Helen Lewis
Senior editor Céline Hughes
Designer Arielle Gamble
Production James Finan and Vincent Smith
Food & prop stylist Kirsty Cassidy
Home economist Nick Banbury

First published in 2014 by
Quadrille Publishing Limited
www.quadrille.co.uk

Text © 2014 Tori Haschka
Photography © 2014 Chris Chen
Design and layout © 2014 Quadrille Publishing Limited

The rights of the author have been asserted.

This edition was published by The Countryman Press,

P.O. Box 748, Woodstock, VT 05091

Distributed by W. W. Norton & Company, Inc., 500 Fifth Avenue, New York, NY 10110

Printed in China

978 1 58157 298 8

My love goes to the friends who helped test recipes, in particular Tristan, Sharon, May, Alice, Melissa M, and Ted, and to the others who so kindly chipped in with "Willwatch" while I cooked and scrawled notes in a notebook.

Lastly, to my family: thank you for helping me believe that anything is possible, and for your support in making it so.

The publisher would like to thank the following ceramicists for their kind loan of props for the photoshoots:

David Edmonds, www.davidedmonds.com.au

Chinaclay, www.chinaclay.com.au

The FortyNine Studio, www.thefortynine.com.au

Sian Thomas, www.sianthomas.net

Joanna Gambatto, Sweet Potato Ceramics,
    www.sweetpotato.net.au

Yew Kong Tham, www.ginkgoleaf.com.au

A note on the recipes

Timings are guidelines for conventional ovens. If you are using a fan-assisted oven, set your oven temperature to approximately 25°F lower. Use an oven thermometer to check the temperature.